Pentland Walks

SWANSTON COTTAGE.

Pentland Walks

WITH THEIR

Literary and Historical Associations

COMPILED AND EDITED BY

ROBERT COCHRANE

Editor of
"The English Essayists," "Great Thinkers and Workers," "Scenes and Memories on the Gareloch,"
"Beneficent and Useful Lives," etc., etc.

With General Map, Illustrations,
and Route Maps

BY

GEORGE SHAW AITKEN

" From Halkerside, from topmost Allermuir,
Or steep Caerketton, dreaming, gaze again."
R. L. Stevenson.

EDINBURGH
ANDREW ELLIOT, 17 PRINCES STREET
And all Booksellers
1908

IN PENTLAND WINE

BY

WILL. H. OGILVIE.

Up here with the wind in our faces,
 And the brown heath under our feet,
We look through the shimmering spaces
 Over tower and steeple and street
To the Lion splendidly sleeping,
 To the tall Crags silent and grey,
To the Castle its grim guard keeping,
 And the shining shield of the Bay.

Behind us the mists of the valley
 Lie low on the moorland's breast,
With the bonnie banks of Bonaly
 In the grey of the winter dressed.
The west wind, wanton, is chiding
 Glencorse with the scourge of his whips,
And the wild ducks over it riding
 Are tossing like storm-tossed ships.

Up here with the clean winds blowing,
 I look to you, City of mine,
I fill me a goblet o'erflowing
 And pledge you in Pentland wine !
With a full heart thrilled by your story,
 While the hills stand round like kings,
I drink to your lasting glory
 In the wine that the hill-wind brir

Reminiscent of a walk with the poet in November 190. m onaly to
Glencorse, by Castlelaw, and Easter Howgate to Edinburgh. A slightly
different version of this poem appeared in the *Scotsman.*—R. C.

PREFACE.

I T was mainly gratitude for health and exhilaration gained from many a Pentland ramble, that prompted the gathering of the literary and historical material given here, together with the desire to hand it on to others who might be likewise interested. Should the book prove suggestive and useful to Pentland pedestrians, its main purpose will be accomplished. Whether or not Edinburgh shall ever, as has been suggested, have proprietory rights over a few thousands of acres on the Pentlands as a public park, the meek and quiet spirits that love the great, simple, beautiful shows of hill, valley, streamlet, can still, by using roads and rights-of-way, enter into their inheritance, none making them afraid. Each eye sees what it brings the power of seeing, and that which helps the never-ending education from common things. Every pedestrian who uses the Pentland paths must feel grateful for what has been done by the Scottish Rights-of-Way Society, in marking out the paths by means of posts, in conserving the public rights therein, and for the pioneer red booklet, "The Pentland Hills, their Paths and Passes," by W. A. S.

To Mr George S. Aitken, architect, belongs the credit of the clear and accurate route maps, on a somewhat novel principle, which it is hoped may prove to be handy and easy of consultation. Mr Aitken has also collaborated with the Editor in regard to the topographical details of some of the routes, and has been otherwise helpful. Hearty acknowledgments are also due to the

Editor of *Chambers's Journal* for permission to use portions of three contributions, and to the Editor of the *Scotsman* for portions of two articles in the *Scotsman*, all by the present writer; to Mrs Hodgson for the description of Bonaly from her husband's memoir; to Mr John Geddie and the representatives of the Riverside Press, for the "Old Lanark Road" chapter from the "Water of Leith, from its Source to the Sea." Also to Mr Will. H. Ogilvie, for his poem "In Pentland Wine." Dr B. N. Peach, late of the Geological Survey, has kindly revised and re-written some portions of the Pentland Geology chapters, originally prepared for the excursions of the British Association when last in Edinburgh. This revision and these additions bring the matter abreast of the latest surveys of the Pentlands. Dr Peach has also added a valuable contribution on the "Development of the Pentlands," and regarding the effect of the "melt-waters" of the ice sheet—the outcome of a lifetime's experience and thought on the subject. The list of Pentland Birds, by Mr R. A. Cochrane, has been revised and supplemented by Mr W. Eagle Clarke, keeper of the Natural History Department, Royal Scottish Museum, and one of the most eminent authorities on the subject. There is a full Bibliography for those who wish to read more extensively; and for Botany E. O. Sonntag's "Pocket Flora of Edinburgh" is mentioned, a book recommended by Professor Bayley Balfour.

Thanks are also due to those who have shown their interest in the book in various practical ways; to Dr David Patrick, Editor of "Chambers's Encyclopædia," who has read proofs; to Mr William Anderson, architect, Mr Malcolm Scott, registrar, Currie, and Mr J. Falconer, who have also assisted in this way. Most of the pictures are from Mr Falconer's excellent photographs.

R. C.

CONTENTS.

Contents

Contents

Pentland Walks

EDINBURGH

Broxburn · Kirkliston · Corstorphine · Ratho · Currie · Balerno · Colinton · Juniper Green · Kirknewton

PENTLAND HILLS

Penicuik · Carlops · West Linton · Dolphinton · Eddleston

Scale

0   1   2   3   4   5 Miles

W. & A. K. Johnston, Limited, Edinburgh & London

Pentland Walks.

CHAPTER I.

Pleasures of Hill Walking—Area of the Pentlands—Sir Walter Scott, Lord Cockburn, James Ballantine, and R. L. Stevenson, on the Pentlands—How to reach the Pentlands—Inns and Tea-Rooms.

PLEASURES OF HILL-WALKING.

IT seems evident that the present passion for golf or cycling, and the desire for being easily and swiftly conveyed from one point to another by motor-car, tram, or rail, militate against the gloriously recreative pastime of hill-walking, which combines gentle and ungentle exercise with bracing air and noble views. With or without company, a hill-walk is one of the good things of this life which inspires towards what is best in nature and human nature. Provided the ground be dry, such a walk is as good in winter as in summer. Dwellers in Edinburgh especially, and rural Midlothian, are fortunate in having the "Pentlands' long line softening into blue" close at hand, "like a wedge of wild nature and old romance thrust into the heart of a workaday

Bonaly Tower.

world." No track of wheels crosses them throughout their length, and sometimes to the tired pedestrian the railway seems to keep a too respectful distance. Pentland memories are of many kinds,

A

homely and heroic, literary and historic, humorous and tragic, and here we recall the more interesting and important of them.

AREA OF THE PENTLANDS.

The eastern and Edinburgh end of the Pentland range is best known, and has been more glorified by poets and litterateurs than where the western slopes sink gently toward the Clyde valley. Their undulating blue lines are so homelike to the returning wanderer, and in parting seem to say, " I will haunt you, you will never forget me."

The name is believed to have been derived from Petland or Pictland. On the east this fine range starts four miles south-west of Edinburgh, and extends westward through the counties of Midlothian, Peebles, and Lanark, for about sixteen miles to near Carnwath, where they slope into Clydesdale. Their average breadth is from four to six miles, broken up by fine ravines and hollows, the principal passes being the Cauldstane Slap between West Linton and Midcalder, passing between East and West Cairn Hills, and Glencorse on the south-east. The highest points are Carnethy (1890 feet) and Scald Law (1898 feet), which rise from the old Biggar road, nine miles south-west from Edinburgh.

The range embraces within its area the peak, the precipice, and the rounded or broad-shouldered hills, forming valleys, the birthplace of many streams, affording delightful walks happily available to the wise pedestrian who may choose, as befits his walking powers, between the four-mile route from Colinton to Glencorse, or the eight-mile one between the Lanark road and West Linton, enjoying in varied directions views of river, strath and wood ; the Forth, the Ochils, and the Grampians ; not least that of " mine own romantic town."

SCOTT, COCKBURN, BALLANTINE, AND R. L. STEVENSON, ON THE PENTLANDS.

Sir Walter Scott, with his unerring eye for the picturesque and wonderful descriptive power, after a drive at sunset between Lasswade and Edinburgh, wrote : " I think I never saw anything more beautiful than the ridge of Carnethy against a clear frosty sky, with its peaks and varied slopes. The hills glowed like purple amethyst; the sky glowed topaz and vermilion colours. I never saw a finer series than Pentland, considering that it is neither rocky nor highly elevated." To Lord Cockburn the competitors for the first prize amongst hills were only—Ben Lomond, Dumyat, and Caerketton, above Swanston. He balanced the claims of each, and his judicial mind, considering the beauty of Edinburgh and the dignity imparted to scenery by objects of importance, was inclined to give the palm to Pentlands. The fact that R. L. Stevenson lived when a lad with his father and mother in the hamlet of Swanston, below Caerketton, accounts for the sketches of the shepherd and the garden in his "Memories and Portraits," the delightful description in "Edinburgh: Picturesque Notes," and many references in his letters and some of his stories, such as "St Ives." He remembered the spot, above the Shearers' Knowe at Swanston, whence the nameless trickle to supply the water-filters comes, where he sat and made bad verses. The Pentlands, says Mr John Geddie, may lay claim to be the birthplace of the genius of R. L. Stevenson; they were his study and class-room, and at Swanston he believes the awakening took place.

James Ballantine tries to express in verse the sights and sounds of a summer day on the hills :—

> "Those airy tones that lightly float
> Seem bursting from the linnet's throat;
> Anon, afar the shy cuckoo
> Soothes with his strain the lone curlew;
> The grasshopper, with elfin drum,
> Beats time unto the wild bee's hum;
> And, with a low sweet music, fills
> Each fairy nook of Pentland Hills.
>
> But, lo! the cadence louder swells—
> The chimes of fair Edina's bells,
> Far in the distance, wake the ear;
> Anon they burst in fulness near,
> And o'er grey crag and valley green,
> Each tiny leaf is dancing seen,
> And every streamlet gurgling trills
> In joy amid the Pentland Hills."

Allan Ramsay, at the beginning of one of his imitations of Horace, gives a winter picture, when neither golf nor bowling are possible :—

> " Look up to Pentland's tow'ring taps,
>   Buried beneath big wreaths o' snaw,
> O'er ilka cleugh, ilk scar an' slap,
>   As high as ony Roman wa'.
>
> Driving their ba's frae whins or tee,
>   There's no ae gowfer to be seen ;
> Nor douser fowk, wysing a-jee
>   The byas bowls on Tamson's green."

HOW TO REACH THE PENTLANDS.

We give here a good deal of material about the skirts of the Pentlands. For those who wish to get upon the hills at once, time is saved in going and returning, by reference to map and railway time-table, and so fixing on the stations nearest the various routes. The Balerno branch of the Caledonian Railway from Princes Street Station, gives ready access to the north side of the Pentlands from Colinton, Juniper Green, Currie, or Balerno. The station of Midcalder, on the main line, suits for the Cauldstane Slap route, with train back from Broomlee (West Linton), at the south end. Of course this and all other routes may be reversed. Harburn Station gives access to the Lang Whang, and the western routes. Dolphinton may be reached circuitously by either Caledonian or North British Railway. There is a poor service of trains for Glencorse and Penicuik. During the summer months motors run to Carlops. For those who cycle, the experience of a day run, all round the hills, is given at the end. It is possible also to cycle, as the writer has done, by Flotterstone Bridge and Glencorse to Loganlee ; push the cycle through the pass which leads to Bavelaw Castle, negotiating two stiles, and so to Balerno. Meanwhile, for those who wish an afternoon or evening walk, there is nothing finer in or near Edinburgh than the route by Morningside to Hillend, or Swanston. The tramways extend to a little beyond Braid Hills Hotel on this route ; on Colinton Road, to near Craiglockhart Skating Pond. The golf courses on

the skirts of the Pentlands, besides the Braids and Morton Hall,
are Lothian Burn ; Glencorse at Milton Bridge, near Penicuik ;
and West Linton, on the south side. On the north, Craiglockhart
Hill, Baberton, Torphin, and King's Knowe.

INNS AND TEA-ROOMS.

For half-day or short excursions, the train from Princes Street
Station, giving access to the stations in Water of Leith valley,
provides the most easily available routes. There are inns or tea-
rooms at Colinton, Juniper Green, Currie, Balerno, and Kirk-
newton on the north side : at Penicuik, Nine-Mile-Burn, Carlops,
and West Linton on the south. On the Biggar road, after Braid
Hills Hotel, until Nine-Mile-Burn or Carlops is reached, there is
no place of refreshment.

View from Rullion Green.

CHAPTER II.

Route 1.

MORNINGSIDE TO SWANSTON.

An easily accomplished Pentland ramble is that to Swanston, the
tiny hamlet associated with R. L. Stevenson, nestling at the north
base of Caerketton, and consisting of a farmhouse, schoolhouse,
Swanston Cottage, and a few cottages.   For this route there is the
tramway for those who wish it to the city boundary at Braid Hills,
and Morningside Station on the Suburban Railway.   But as there
is much of interest in the Morningside suburb in our walk from
Bruntsfield, we note a few of the interesting features.

If we care to imagine a native of Edinburgh, who had been
absent for a time from the town, again revisiting the suburb of
Morningside, he would find but few of the older landmarks in
existence.   The low cottages which lined the right and left of
Morningside Road are, with a few exceptions, swept away, and
have given place to high tenements, with a double line of busy
tramway between, and a much too narrow roadway and pavements
for such an important avenue citywards.   A jumble of houses
meets the eye to right and left, filling the sides and bottom of
the descending and rising ground, sweeping up to the border of

the Braid Burn, and even wandering out beyond, along the old and new Biggar roads.

EMINENT FORMER RESIDENTS.

In the big square villa at the north-west end of Church Hill, marked by a tablet, died Dr Chalmers. Close to Morningside Parish Church is the Bore-Stone, a block of sandstone on which the flagstaff of the Royal Standard was planted, when King James IV. mustered his army on the Borough-muir in 1513. To the east are Wood Grove, and Wood-ville, in Canaan Lane, the last once the residence of Christopher North's naturalist brother James Wilson; Millbank, the residence of Professor Syme; Canaan Lodge (now rebuilt), associated with Dr Gregory, whose name still survives in connection with his famous "mixture." The site of St Roque's Chapel lay further east. The old school remains in Morningside Road, but the gate pillars of Falcon Hall adorn another entrance in the Corstorphine Road. The hammer of the destroyer has removed Falcon Hall, the grounds around which might

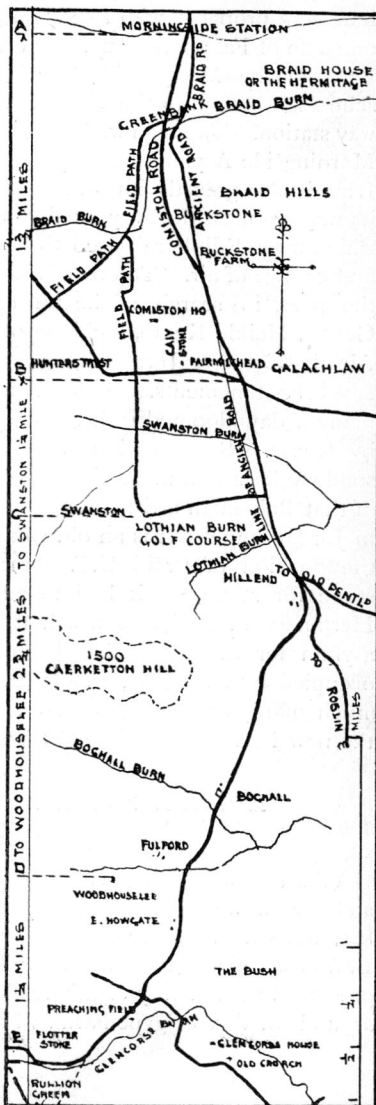

ROUTE NO. 1.

have made an admirable public park for the district. The brand new tenement property, with St Peter's Roman Catholic Church, form one side of Falcon Avenue. There are four more churches southward in the Morningside district, one public and two private schools, a branch of the Free Library, a hotel, cemetery, and railway station. The high wall and prison-like gateway to East House, Morningside Asylum, have given way to high tenements; Canaan Lane is also graced with some tenement property which has edged its way amongst the cosy, quaint suburban residences, to come to which from Edinburgh used to mean a most delightful rural walk and change of air. To one of these cottages came Sydney Dobell, the poet, in search of health and quiet; and the funeral of George Meikle Kemp, architect of the Scott Monument, was from Ainslie Cottage, Jordan Lane, which is still standing, though faced by tenements. Bloomsberry Cottage, Canaan Lane, for many a day bloomed with roses, and was a residence of and built by Kemp. Some curious carved stones are built here in the stable walls, and a memorial stone with Latin inscription. Stories of that Bohemian artist, Sam Bough, still linger around his cottage in Jordan Lane. It is an old story how the tollhouse (in line with the position of Braid U.F. Church) was removed, and rebuilt stone for stone, as it had stood, at the entrance gate to the Hermitage of Braid, of which it now forms the lodge. A new asylum for the insane has been built at old Craighouse, once occupied by Dr Lizars, and later by John Hill Burton, who did much of his literary work there. Craiglockhart Poorhouse and the new Fever Hospital lie to the south-west.

MODERN MORNINGSIDE, CRAIGHOUSE HILL.

Villas, semi-detached villas, and tenement property jostle one another on the east side of Craighouse Hill to the right. To the left, the care and surveillance exercised by the trustees of the Braid estate have kept the speculative builder in his place, and preserved the amenity of this really fine district, built on the fields around what was Egypt Farm, which stood just where Nile Grove intersects Woodburn Terrace. Thus rapidly has the ground been covered with villas and semi-detached villa property.

Plewlands House, now removed, on the slope of Craighouse Hill, stood in solitary state, and beyond it Craighouse. There is a secret passage at Craighouse which has been explored by some folks who are still living. Craighouse once belonged to the family of Sir William Dick, Knight of Braid, whose romantic story is told in Smith's "Grange of St Giles."

Miss Warrender, in her charming "Walks Round Edinburgh," hints at a Covenanting origin for the Biblical nomenclature in Morningside. There is another suggestion. Mrs Fletcher, wife of a well known Edinburgh advocate, came out from Edinburgh with her husband and children in 1799 to Egypt Farm. "Mr Fletcher's health as well as my own," she says, "seeming to require change of air, we repaired with our children to a very inexpensive cottage in the Morningside district, to the south of Edinburgh, called Egypt, so named in memory of a gipsy colony who, as tradition said, had their headquarters in the immediate neighbourhood, by virtue of a grant of land from one of the Scottish Kings." There is still another suggestion : Cromwell's camp in 1650-51 was on the south side of the Braids, and the soldiers described the fighting as "Joshua against the Canaanites." Men with Biblical expressions constantly on their lips were equal to the starting of a Biblical series of names.

THE GORDONS OF CLUNY.

An ornate, covered tomb in St Cuthbert's Churchyard encloses the dust of the old lairds of the Braid estate, the Gordons of Cluny Castle in Aberdeenshire. Former proprietors were the Fairlies, Dicks, and Browns. Maitland derives the name Hermitage from a "hermit's cell originally at that place." Charles Gordon, who bought the Braid estate about 1771, died 15th May 1814. The next heir, Colonel John Gordon, died 16th July 1858 ; and his son, John Gordon, died 31st March 1878. The widow of John Gordon of Cluny, Emily Elizabeth Steele, grand-daughter of Sir John Pringle of Stitchill, married, on December 5, 1880, Sir

Reginald Archibald Edward Cathcart, captain in the Coldstream Guards. It has, therefore, been under the regime of Sir Reginald and Lady Gordon Cathcart that the Braid estate has emerged from yielding a mere agricultural rent to be valuable suburban property.

PLAN OF OLD MORNINGSIDE.

An old plan enables us to get a bird's-eye view of the Braid estate and Morningside as it was in 1772. It is entitled "A Plan of the Barony of Braid, with the Hermitage and Policie, the property of Charles Gordon, Esq., Surveyed July 1772 by John Home." Between Jordan Burn and Braid Burn only some half a dozen houses are shown; dwellings appear opposite to what is now Hermitage Terrace; there is the farm of Egypt, and Braid Burn Cottages, near the bridge over the Braid Burn, with Over Braid Farm; while Greenbank, Plewlands, and Craighouse, being outside the scope of the map, are not shown, although the farm road to the latter from the "Moffat Road" is indicated. This Moffat Road is the Braid Road, with a second milestone from Tollcross marked near Braid Burn Cottages. The corresponding first milestone may still be seen built into the wall opposite Morningside Parish Church. On the main road a bridge is indicated over the Jordan, and a farm road runs almost parallel with what is the present Suburban Railway, from near where the station stands, to Egypt; another road strikes east from the Edinburgh road, which joins one coming from Braid, and also goes to Egypt. There was then either a path or road, indicated as "Road to Blackford, Edinburgh, &c.," running along the north side of Blackford. The total extent of Braid estate was 412 acres; names of tenants mentioned are George Tennant, Widow Dick, and Peter Hardie. "Lands of Canaan" are indicated in what is now Woodburn Terrace; the Braid Hills Road is called "Road to the Coals, Liberton, &c." There is a mill and a dam indicated in the bed of the Braid Burn, with a "Mill Acre," as also a "Pool," and five small lochs are marked alongside the Braid Hills Road to Liberton. The ground around where Morningside Cemetery is now laid out is marked "Mr Seivewright's Lands." Some names on the Braid

Hills are " Black Suck," " Gouck Folds," " Liff Loch,' " Long Den Rigs," and " White Rig Fauld."

PLEWLANDS.

Sir Thomas Dick Lauder, in his delightful book " Scottish Rivers," gives a sketch of the Jordan Burn, which now runs in a conduit past Nile Grove, from its rise in Craighouse Hill till it joins the Braid Burn, and indulges in some prose poetry over Blackford House further east ; and the Rev. Robert Morehead, D.D., at one time Dean of Edinburgh, and one of the ministers of St Paul's, York Place, felt enthusiastic when resident at Plewlands, at the top or west side of what is now Morningside Cemetery. This farmhouse was one of the few remaining links with older Morningside, but it too is gone, and buildings now cover the slope of Craighouse Hill. The Ordnance Survey Map of 1853 marks " ruins " to the east of Plewlands, and Dick Lauder writes of the " remains of an ancient castle or tower very much en-cumbered by the modern buildings of a farm." He looked into the ruined, dilapidated apartments, and thought with pity of those who had been condemned to live in them. Dr Morehead wrote of the atmosphere of the place in June 1823, " A most beautiful summer residence near Braid, where I am alone with my daughter Isabella. In the mornings I study Hebrew. I sometimes think of writing my journal here in blank verse. There is a great deal of poetry scattered about me, if I could catch it, and it is a pity to lose the power of versification. The poetry of life is the only poetry it is worth preserving. But I shall not strike it out from prose this morning." Sir Walter Scott used to quote some lines of Dr Morehead's on the Eildon Hills, beginning thus :—

> " Calm slept the clouds on cloven Eildon laid,
> And distant Melrose peered from leafy shade,"

to his visitors at Abbotsford, and then ask the authorship. Professor Wilson admired his Pentland series of sonnets, and one would like to know if these still exist.

EARLY WATER SUPPLIES.

Morningside has been associated with the first and last of Edinburgh's water schemes. Lately a connection was made there with the new Talla pipes of the Water Trust. From this district came the early water supply of Edinburgh. Peter Brusche, a German plumber, was paid about £3000 for laying a lead pipe, 3 inches in diameter, from Comiston to the reservoir at Castle-hill. This was in 1681; by 1720 a pipe of 4½ inches was required and laid; there was an increase of size again in 1785, and in 1790 an iron pipe of 7 inches diameter was laid from Swanston to the town, and the additional water from Comiston was thus brought in at a cost of £20,000.

TO SWANSTON BY COMISTON.

Just beyond Morningside Station, 2½ miles from the G.P.O., there is a choice of ways : that by the old Braid Road to the left, and by Comiston Road following the tram lines straight forward by an easy gradient. These unite beyond Buckstone.

At Greenbank, on the Comiston Road, we pass the entrance lodges to Craiglockhart Poorhouse and the Fever Hospital to the right, and beyond, a pleasant path strikes off, which winds by hedgerow and through fields to Comiston, and so to Swanston, passing Comiston House on the left, and Hunter's Tryst on the right. This last was once a howff of the Six Foot Club, of which Scott and Hogg were members. In addition, it had the reputation of being haunted. To-day it is profitably haunted by cows as a dairy. There is a scene in "St Ives" located here by Stevenson. Behind are the woods of Dreghorn. The path at the right in crossing the Braid Burn leads to Dreghorn. If we keep the tram line and Penicuik road to Fairmilehead, or choose to follow the older Braid Road, we have charming views from both, westwards, beyond Dalmahoy Hill, with the Pentlands southwards. At night the lights of Broxburn may be seen. On a clear day, from Fairmilehead, the hills of Fife, the Ochils, and Ben Ledi may be descried. R. L. Stevenson wandered to and from Swanston by the footpath past Comiston Farm, and with the down-droop of his head and careless attire was thought by native or passer-by " to be no a' there."

STORY OF THE BRAID ROAD ROBBERY.

The old Braid Road, starting near Morningside Station on the left, has associations of its own. Volunteers practised shooting at targets on Blackford Hill from a field here. The robbery of David Loch, the Biggar carrier, in Braid Road, 3rd November 1814, led to the hanging of two miscreants on Wednesday, 25th January 1815, just where the deed was committed. The stones, which provided a socket for a gibbet, may still be seen in Braid Road, a little south from the U.F. Church. David Loch was riding on horseback from Biggar to Edinburgh, and had passed Buckstone and Brigs o' Braid, when near a solitary thorn-bush two men stopped him, and one of them asked him the time. Loch slackened his pace, said " he didna ken, but believed it wad be about six." " Sure enough," said the one who had not spoken, " it is as near eleven." The carrier took them for two drunk countrymen, but was soon undeceived, when one of them rushed forward, seized the bridle, while the other dragged him from his horse. The two were upon him with their knees in a moment, and in the struggle several of his ribs were broken. Loch shouted " Murder, murder!" as loudly as he could. One of the men struck him several blows on the head with the butt-end of a pistol, and threatened further to knock his brains out, if he were not quiet. Loch kept crying, " O dear!" which secured the attention of Andrew Black, blacksmith, of Braidburn, who was passing at the moment. He rescued Loch from the ditch, and took him to the farm of Myreside. The two Irishmen, Thomas Kelly and Henry O'Neill, scuttled across the fields, having emptied Loch's pockets of all his money. Later they were apprehended in a house in the West Port. The prosecution would probably have failed had it not been for a leather purse containing a few shillings which was found on the robbers. The carrier was asked in Court if he could identify it as his. " Yes," he said, "my wife put three steeks in the corner of it before I left home," and sure enough when handed round there were the steeks, and the fate of the two men was sealed. They were suspected of having robbed Mr Dewar of Vogrie, a short time previously, and were hanged here, where the robbery took place. This was the last case in Scotland of hanging for highway robbery.

HERMITAGE OF BRAID.

Sir John Skelton, the apologist for Queen Mary and biographer of Lethington, lived and wrote and died at Hermitage. Sir John has left memorials of some of the noted people, such as J. A. Froude, Professor Blackie, Jowett, Huxley, Sellar, Sir Noel Paton, and others, who visited the Hermitage.

OLD MILLS ON BRAID BURN.

A case which went to the House of Lords, 30th March 1789, gives information about the Braid estate. In the evidence it transpires that Charles Gordon, in the spring of 1785, built a new house on this estate at a very considerable expense, "from the predilection of its beauty and situation."

The appellants were Major George Ramsay of Peffermill, and Charles Gordon, Esquire of Braid, against the Lord Provost and Magistrates, who proposed to increase the water supply from the Braid Burn, to the prejudice of the mills at Braid, Peffermill, and Duddingston. All the evidence went to show that Braid Mill was driven by a gathered dam in summer and in frost, and that the upper dam took sometimes two days to fill in a dry season. The rental of Braid Mill was £25 a year; of Peffermill and Bleachfield, £45; and of Duddingston, £100 a year, exclusive of the coal and salt works, the annual profits of which are stated at ten times that sum.

SCOTT AND BURNS ON THE BRAIDS.
A MEMORY OF THE '45.

Scott's fine lines on Edinburgh from the Braids are well known. One would fain believe that when Burns was having an early

morning stroll with Dugald Stewart on the Braids, it was a distant
prospect of some smoking cottages which gave such pleasure to
his mind, a pleasure he said none could understand who had
not witnessed the like himself, because of the happiness and
worth they contained.   And no doubt the walk with Painter
Nasmyth to the Pentlands, straight from a High Street tavern, at
3 A.M., was by this route.   It was then that the poet was frightened by a lunatic in a cottage.   They came down from the hills
to Roslin for breakfast.   Forty-two years earlier, when Prince
Charlie's men were taking possession of Edinburgh, as recorded
in "The Woodhouselee MS." of Mr C. E. S. Chambers, the
Whig Laird saw the cavalcade "and all the Highland wifes"
along with the baggage of that irregular army pass here.   "They
crossed the Linton Road I was walking along to Edinburgh.   . .
I crossed their road after they had past Morton, and came up
with ane honest farmer in Collington Mains, whose horses and
carriages they had pressed.   He told me they had plundered and
broke all his furniture, they had robbed 6 silver spoons.   I took
off the by-road to Brade, and went down to Canaan Muir, and at
a distance had a politer sight.   This was the pretended Prince,
his retinue, and guards."   The Prince, we are told, stopped at
Grange House, and had some wine ; kept out of range of the
Castle guns, and so to Holyrood.   After Prestonpans the same
scribe notes, November 5, 1745, "I returned from Edinburgh, at
Buckstain I met from Swanston, a set of country men carrying in
three Highlanders, and using them not tenderly, but the gang
have irritated the country by their pilfering and oppression,
and they are seized everywhere, and taken to the Castle of
Edinburgh."

THE BUCK-STONE.

The old road descends to the Braid Burn at Hermitage Gate,
and passes the lodge built of the stones of the old Morningside
Toll Bar, and an exact facsimile.   As we go southward we pass Braid
Hills Road, and on the right hand, opposite the Mortonhall Golf
Club House, the rock in a wall known as the "Buck-Stone,"
a large fragment, on which the proprietor of the Barony of

Penicuik is bound by his tenure to sit and wind three blasts of a horn when the King shall come to hunt on the Boroughmuir. Hence the crest of the Clerks of Penicuik—a demi-forester proper, winding a horn, with the motto, " Frie for a blast." Scott gives this tradition in a note to his " Gray Brother." Maitland, in his " History of Edinburgh," relates this regarding the Bore Stone near Church Hill, and the Buck-Stone, he says, was thus named because the King's buck-hounds were unchained here.

The Buck-Stone.

Some stone cists were found on the highest point of the Braids about the middle of last century. A little further on is the junction of the two roads, and opposite, on the right hand, an extensive deposit of sand—an indication of long-past water action. Here is the entrance to Comiston House, which was built in 1815. On the estate are the remains of an old dovecot, suggesting an even older house.

MORTON HALL—CROMWELL'S CAMP.

At Fairmilehead four roads meet. That to the east leads to Morton House, where John Hill Burton, the historian, died in

1881.   Morton House, like Morton Hall, which lies further east, belonged, in James III.'s time, to Sir Oliver Sinclair.   When the estate belonged to Sir Oliver Sinclair of Roslin, about 1486, it was attached to the Barony of Pentland.   The founder of the Trotter family of Mortonhall was John Trotter, a benevolent Edinburgh merchant, who sprang from a Berwickshire family.   Galachlaw, the southward-sloping ridge from the Braids, between Mortonhall on the east and Fairmilehead on the west, is mentioned as a place where Cromwell encamped before the battle of Dunbar.   The month of

Old Stone, Comiston Lodge.

August 1650 was exceptionally wet, and some 2000 were on the sick list.   "Blessed be God," ran a sentence in a letter next year, "we have now other shelter and footing than Pentland Hills," which was the name given by the soldiers to the Braids, Blackford, Craiglockhart, and Colinton neighbourhood.   There was no timber here at that time : they had to erect a gallows for a sergeant who had looted a cloak, but "there was no tree to hang him on."   The ground for the water filters of the Edinburgh Water Trust lies to the left of Fairmilehead : the main water pipes from Talla turn down Mortonhall road to Alnwick Hill.

The pipes are on the left of the road all the way to Flotterstone Bridge, Glencorse. The Roman Watling Street from the south also passed here to Cramond. The road from Lothianburn follows the military way for a mile, and here Roman coins were found.

Moving westwards, on the right is a whinstone block, 11 feet high, in a field, set edgewise, north and south, and supposed to mark the scene of an ancient battle, as, when the road along which we are passing was formed, many stone cists were found, with skeletons within them. The stone, however, may indicate a point of outlook, as very extensive views, north and south, are to be had from its site. It is known as the Caiy Stone, or battle stone. The Camus Stone, from which the name Comiston is derived, has disappeared from this neighbourhood, as have also two other conical cairns. In a rabbit-burrow on Lothian Burn Golf Course a burial urn was unearthed a few years ago.

The Caiy Stone.

SWANSTON.

We now reach the road going south to Swanston, and note before us the ruddy screes of Caerketton, and the T-shaped wood which marks the position of the picturesque hamlet of Swanston, and of Swanston Cottage to the right, where, for about a dozen summers, lived R. L. Stevenson, making it the centre of his Pentland rambles. Swanston Farm had an open door for the Covenanters—hungry visitors coming down from the hills towards the dresser, which was laden with bread, cheese, bannocks, milk, and brandy. The farm was originally a Grange of Whitekirk Abbey, which after the Reformation came into Protestant hands, and is now the property of the Trotters of Morton Hall.

Stevenson was remembered quite well by Mrs Ochiltree, who occupied a small shop in a whitewashed cottage. He always lifted his hat to her in passing. The Stevenson carriage would stop at the toll-house at Fairmilehead when the family were passing and repassing from Edinburgh to Swanston, and many a dainty was left for Mrs Ochiltree's husband. There is a memorial to Stevenson in St Giles's Church : a monument-fountain has been erected to his memory in San Francisco ; a fountain might well be erected to his memory at Swanston, now quite a place of pilgrimage.

ASSOCIATIONS WITH STEVENSON.

Sir John Skelton mentions having walked over from Hermitage of Braid to Swanston Cottage with Principal Tulloch, to dine with the Stevensons. R. L. S., then only a lad, was absent ; but his mother, who treasured every scrap of his writing, gave the two visitors away some juvenile contributions to local journals. Both agreed that here was a fresh voice, with a note delicate and unborrowed as the lark's. Skelton was not sure if he ever did anything better than some of these early trifles.

After the "Pentland Rising" booklet of 1866, the literary fruitage of R. L. Stevenson's life, before he became a fixture at Vailima, Samoa, was shed at all sorts of places. He had also seen all kinds of life. In the days of what he calls his green-sickness, in the sanded kitchen of an Edinburgh public house, he had met seamen, chimney-sweeps, and thieves. Once he wrote to his mother : "I must be a bit of a vagabond : it's your own fault after all, isn't it? You shouldn't have had a tramp for a son." By 1886 he had slept in forty-six English towns, fifty in Scotland, seventy-four in France, and forty in the rest of Europe. But the fancy and imagination of R. L. Stevenson continued to hover over well-remembered scenes in Edinburgh, Swanston, and the Pentlands to the very last ; and many of his letters, when any of his old haunts are alluded to, seem to end in a longing sigh, as in some of the last lines he wrote :

> "I gang nae mair where ance I gaed,
> By Buckstone, Fairmilehead, or Braid,

But far frae Kirk and Tron.
Oh, still, ayont the muckle sea,
Still are ye dear, and dear to me,
Auld Reekie, still and on."

"It is a singular thing," he writes, "that I should live here in the South Seas, under conditions so new and so striking, and yet my imagination so continually inhabit the cold old huddle of grey hills from which we came." The three fine verses Crockett received in acknowledgment of the dedication of the "Stickit

Cottages at Swanston.

Minister" to the Exile of Samoa, beginning, "Blows the wind to-day," breathe the same feeling. And from far Samoa he wrote :

"The tropics vanish ; and meseems that I—
From Halkerside, from topmost Allermuir,
Or steep Caerketton—dreaming, gaze again."

The whole panorama rose up before that "inward eye which is the bliss of solitude." There was the town, like an island in the smoke, cragged, spired, and turreted ; new folds of the city glitter on seaward-dropping hills. The Forth gleams beyond, and Fife smokes with scores of towns. He thinks of the New Calton burying-ground, where rest his father's ashes, and those of his friends, and he conjures up the lighthouses and breakwaters built by the Stevensons of lighthouse fame. The voice of generations of dead called to him to arise—but, alas, this was not to be—to retrace his footsteps, and stretch himself down in that "devoted city of the dead."

"He was just naething when I kenned him," said the worthy woman in whose "ben" had died John Todd, the "Roaring Shepherd," whose likeness figures in "Memories and Portraits." The old Scottish Gardener is another Swanston reminiscence, and how lovingly Stevenson describes the place in his "Edinburgh : Picturesque Notes."

SWANSTON COTTAGE.

In "St Ives," his imagination was playing in and around Swanston, whither he leads one of his characters, and gives an idealised description of Swanston Cottage : "A single gable and chimney of the cottage peered over the shoulder of the hill ; not far off, and a trifle higher on the mountain, a tall old whitewashed farmhouse stood among the trees, beside a falling brook ; beyond were rough hills of pasture. . . . The cottage was a little quaint place of many rough cast gables, and grey roofs. It had something the air of a rambling infinitesimal cathedral, the body of it rising in the midst two storeys high, with a steep pitched roof, and sending out upon all hands (as it were chapter-houses, chapels, and transepts), one-storeyed and dwarfish projections. To add to this appearance, it was grotesquely decorated with crockets and gargoyles, ravished from some mediæval church." Readers of the story will remember the Drove Road, and the meeting with Sir Walter Scott, as St Ives neared the border country.

In the small house at the entrance gate to Swanston Cottage, his nurse, Miss Cunningham, the "Cummy" of the "Child's Garden of Verses," lived for a time.

VIEW FROM CAERKETTON.

There is a very extensive and interesting view from the top of Caerketton, just above Swanston. From its base the land falls and swells to the southern shores of the Firth of Forth, its undulations broken by the ridge of Edinburgh City, the Castle Rock, Calton Hill, and Arthur's Seat. On the northern shore, Kincardine, Donibristle, Aberdour, Burntisland, and Kirkcaldy, all claim notice for their historical or commercial interest. In the far north-west are the Perthshire and northern Grampians, shouldered Ben Lomond, pyramidal Ben Voirlich and Ben Ledi being conspicuous. Nearer are the rounded Ochils, in the centre the Fife Lomonds and Largo Law; due north and beyond them is Dundee Law, which looks down on Dundee City. The view north-eastward is along the coast of East Lothian, to the Bay of Aberlady, with Lord Wemyss's fine house of Gosford standing out white from its woody background. Further east the coast heads in to North Berwick Law; the historical Bass Rock, the home of the sea birds, but a short distance from it. Possibly the eye may light on the ruins of Tantallon Castle, and from them wander in thought to "Marmion," the Braids and Blackford lying nearer at hand, from which Scott gives his hero the vision of the ancient capital. Still eastward is Traprain Law, sacred to the memory of St Kentigern and his mother, St Thenaw (still reverenced in Glasgow as St Enoch); it rises out of the Tyne valley, which is crowned on the south by the long range of the Lammermoors, with Soutra Hill on their western shoulder, marking the ancient line of one of the southern roads.

Distances—Princes Street Station to Flotterstone Bridge, Glencorse, 7 miles. From Tollcross to Braid Hills Car Terminus, 2 miles; to Fairmilehead, 3 miles; Swanston, 4 miles; Hillend, 4 miles; Easter Howgate (Woodhouselee), 6 miles. At Fairmilehead, distance from Edinburgh G.P.O., $4\frac{1}{4}$ miles; to Carlops, $9\frac{3}{4}$ miles; to Penicuik, 6 miles; to Roslin, $4\frac{1}{4}$ miles; to Liberton, $2\frac{1}{2}$ miles; to Dalkeith, 6 miles; to Colinton, $2\frac{1}{4}$ miles.

CHAPTER III.

Route 1 (continued).

FAIRMILEHEAD TO WOODHOUSELEE, RULLION GREEN, AND GLENCORSE.

A Hillend View—Pentland Churchyard—Penicuik and the Paper Industry—
Penicuik Worthies—Memories of the Road—Woodhouselee and the Tytlers
—Old and New Woodhouselee (or Fulford)—The Ghost—Scott at Wood-
houselee—The Highlanders here during the '45—A Summer House—The
Bush—Glencorse Old Kirk—Memories of Glencorse by R. L. Stevenson—
Stevenson's " Pentland Rising "—Rullion Green Martyrs' Monument—
Story of the Rising of 1666—General Drummond describes the Battle—
House of Muir—Mauricewood.

A HILLEND VIEW.

A CART road skirts Lothian Burn golf course, and gives access from
Swanston to the Penicuik Road. Past Lothian Burn, there are
three roads from which to choose. We ascend that to the right
known as the old Biggar Road, where from the higher levels beyond
Hillend, the eastern extremity of the Pentlands, we see eastwards
the sweep of the Firth of Forth, with the Bass and North Berwick
Law. Nearer, Arthur Seat is plainly seen. The hills that guard
Tweedside are to the south-west, the Moorfoots to the south,
running into the Lammermoors. South-east are Dalkeith and
Musselburgh, surrounded by interesting spots of historic interest
such as Fa'side Castle, and Elphinstone Tower, near which is the
field of Carberry, the scene of one of the closing episodes in Queen
Mary's reign. On the banks of the North and South Esk are
Temple Church, Roslin Chapel, Hawthornden, Newbattle Abbey,
Dalkeith Palace, all names which conjure up interesting historical
memories. St Catherine's with its miraculous balm well just south
from Liberton, Gracemount adjoining with its ecclesiastical asso-

ciations, the Inch, Drum, Edmonstone, and many another historical spot, all have some landmark shewing their situation.

At Pentland old churchyard below, on the left, on the Loanhead road, is a massive slab with a floriated cross, unfortunately mutilated. Of the other more recent monuments, one has been a table-stone, on the ends of whose supports are four finely cut figures—a sower, a reaper, an eater, and a flower-gatherer, the last with roses entwined about his body—while on the fifth and central support is a group showing Death as the King of Terrors, crowned and armed with a long spear, preparing to attack a trio of victims—a youth, a seated female figure, and a baby on her knee, the youth vigorously interposing between Death and his prey. Sir John Gibson of Pentland and other members of his family are buried here. Mr James Currie of Pentland was mainly responsible for the erection of the Martyrs' Monument in Greyfriars' Churchyard.

The birthplace of G. M. Kemp, at Moorfoot, is south from here. The whole vale of North Esk before us is redolent with memories of celebrities, from near its rise, at North Esk Reservoir above Carlops. At Newhall Allan Ramsay's "Habbie's Howe" is situated. De Quincey resided for about fifteen years in a cottage known as Mavis Bush, at Polton; then there is Hawthornden, with memories of Drummond; Lasswade, where Scott first set up his household gods after marriage; and near here Mrs Oliphant records she first awoke to consciousness of things around her. Dalkeith has associations with General Monk, the Buccleuch family, and Norman Macleod. Musselburgh, which was a Roman station, has memories of David Macbeth Moir, poet, and author of "Mansie Wauch."

PENICUIK AND THE PAPER INDUSTRY.

To the south-west lies Penicuik, the centre of much that is interesting. Scott in boyhood met the original of "Monkbarns" of the "Antiquary" at Penicuik House. Mr Crockett once occupied Bank House; and Professor Cossar Ewart once conducted his experiments with hybrids on this estate. Paper-making is a considerable industry in Penicuik. The mills were erected between 1773 and 1777, as the first cotton mill built in Scotland, leading to the erection of others at Lanark, but in 1811 the business was given up, and the buildings sold to the Government, for the accommodation of the troops detailed to watch the French prisoners at Valleyfield. After the peace they were bought by Messrs Haig and others, and fitted up with paper-making machinery. In 1821 the firm parted with their interests to James Brown, to whom they had incurred financial obligations. In the hands of Mr Brown, and afterwards of his son-in-law, Mr Thomas M'Dougal, the foundations of the present excellent business were laid. The Valleyfield Mills of Messrs Cowan had their start in 1708 by Mr Andrew Anderson, printer to Queen Anne. In 1773 the mills were acquired by Mr Thomas Boswell, who sold them after six years' occupancy to Mr Charles Cowan, merchant, Leith, ancestor of the present proprietors. Cowan and his two sons, Duncan and Alexander, carried on a moderately successful business with thirty workpeople, turning out two or three tons weekly of hand-made paper. In 1804 the firm bought Penicuik corn-mill, turned it into a paper-mill, and there for some time made paper for bank-notes. In 1811 the Valleyfield Mills were sold to Government as a depôt for French prisoners, about six thousand being confined there. The mills were re-purchased by Mr Cowan in 1818, and since then, by continued extensions where required, and the introduction of the best and latest machinery, the firm have taken front rank in the trade. The output of writing and printing papers at Valleyfield, Bank, and Low Mills is about one hundred tons weekly, and the firm now employ between seven hundred and eight hundred workpeople.

Charles Cowan has, in his privately printed "Reminiscences" (1878), recalled the names of some of those whom he had seen in the house of his father, Alexander Cowan, at 5 St John Street, Edinburgh. There were John, James, and Alexander Ballantyne, who resided at No. 14, the latter a younger son of John Ballantyne, father of John Ballantyne the Artist and of Robert M. Ballantyne the writer of books for boys. A brother of Charles Cowan revised Scott's "Napoleon," and received a set of the volumes with compliments from Scott. One of these volumes was borrowed and never returned, when Charles Cowan intimated that the person who had taken the first volume might call for the other eight !

PENICUIK WORTHIES.

The Penicuik neighbourhood is very healthy, and sick soldiers transferred from Edinburgh to the hospital at Glencorse barracks rapidly recover. Glencorse Station terminus of the N.B.R. branch line is opposite. Mauricewood House is the residence of Dr Joseph Bell, the prototype of "Sherlock Holmes." "The Memoirs of the Life of Sir John Clerk of Penicuik, Baron of Exchequer," have been printed by the Scottish History Society. The founder of the family began life as a Montrose merchant, but made his fortune in Paris, acquired the lands of Penicuik and Wrightshouses, Edinburgh, and died in 1674. Mr Wilson in his "Annals of Penicuik" relates how, at the beginning of last century, a labourer on the farm of Cornbank, at Penicuik, had a son who rose to be Peter Borthwick, M.P., editor of the *Morning Post*, and whose son, Sir Algernon Borthwick, Bart. (Lord Glenesk), is proprietor of that newspaper. The story of the elder Borthwick reads like a romance, from the time he opened an unsuccessful adventure-school at Auchendinny, and during vacation periods attended the United Associate Hall as a student. He became tutor to a young lady who resided with her uncle near the Borders, whom he eventually married. They had a hard, uphill fight ere the lady could legally claim the fortune which was hers. The Presbytery of Edinburgh did not allow him to finish his college course ; and he went to Oxford, where he studied with a view to holy orders, but was unsuccessful. Next he was connected with the London theatres, lectured on slavery, entered Parliament as member for Evesham, and his journalistic career resulted in his connection with the *Morning Post*.

Alexander Keith Johnston was a native of the parish of Penicuik, and Henry Mackenzie lived for several summers at Auchendinny, as did also Mrs Fletcher. "Christopher North" (Professor Wilson) came to Roslin for a time on the death of his wife. The Howgate carrier's house is just across the Esk from Auchendinny, near Pomathorn, where the last scenes in the life of the hero of John Brown's "Rab and his Friends" were enacted. Rosebery, the estate from which Lord Rosebery takes his title, lies to the south-east, near the base of the Moorfoot Hills. Another estate of his lordship's is that of Malleny, on the north side, at Balerno.

MEMORIES OF THE ROAD.

One thinks of the lonely drives of the carrier; the weary coach rides of Thomas Carlyle as a student, by Ericstane and Broughton towards Edinburgh University; or the cheery drives on the Dumfries coach from Princes Street of Christopher North, bent on angling expeditions to Tweedside, beside the Crook, and in Talla Glen. Every Pentland pedestrian thinks of the Covenanters, and of the disaster at Rullion Green in 1666, the subject of R. L Stevenson's virgin booklet. Then Allan Ramsay must have known the Biggar road well, which hugs the south side of the Pentlands.

The late Alexander Ireland has recorded how scores of times Dr Hodgson, Dr Robert Chambers, Robert Cox, and himself had crossed the Pentlands from Woodhouselee, by the Compensation Pond, over to Currie. They used to meet at the head of the links, near Morningside, at 7 a.m., and walk out by Lothianburn to Gilchrist's Inn at Woodhouselee, where they always breakfasted. They had the healthy appetites of pedestrians, and never, said Ireland, "were there better ham and eggs than those of Mrs Gilchrist."

WOODHOUSELEE AND THE TYTLERS.

After passing Boghall farmhouse and Fulford we come, in a delightful nook below Castlelaw, to Woodhouselee. The irregular pile known as Woodhouselee, having a square tower at one corner, originally the old fortalice of Fulford, dating from the fourteenth century, has been in the Tytler family since 1748. The Tytlers were Seatons. How the name was changed and how the founder of the family came across from France in the retinue of Queen Mary is delightfully told, with much else, in the Life of Patrick

Fraser Tytler, the historian of Scotland, by Dean Burgon. The book is most justly styled "The Portrait of a Christian Gentleman." William Tytler, who purchased Woodhouselee, was widely known for a book defending Queen Mary, and his recipe for a happy old age like his own was, "short but cheerful meals, music, and a good conscience." His son, Alexander Tytler, Lord Woodhouselee, published "Elements of General History," and succeeded here and at his Princes Street home in gathering round him the most eminent men of his time in his happy household. His translation of Schiller's "Robbers" helped to direct Scott towards German literature. Amongst his guests, besides Walter Scott, were Professor Dugald Stewart, Lord Jeffrey, Henry Mackenzie, Sydney Smith, Basil Hall, Sir James Stuart of Allanbank, and John Leyden, who wrote the following sonnet with a diamond on a pane of the window in his bedroom, where we read it the other day. The glass is cracked, but the lines are entire. The window looks north on the Pentlands and on the musical hill-burn so besung :

> Sweet rivulet ! as in pensive mood reclined,
>   Thy lone voice talking to the night I hear,
>   Now swelling loud and louder on the ear,
> Now sinking in the pauses of the wind,
> A stilly sadness overspreads my mind,
>   To think how oft the whirling gale shall strew
>   O'er thy bright stream the leaves of sallow hue,
> Ere next this classic haunt my wanderings find.
> That lulling harmony resounds again,
>   That soothes the slumbering leaves on every tree,
>   And seems to say, "Wilt thou remember me?"
> The stream that listened oft to Ramsay's strain,
> Though Ramsay's pastoral reed be heard no more,
> Yet taste and fancy long shall linger on thy shore.

There is an ominous ring in the lines, written before the poet and orientalist left for India in 1802, never to return.

OLD AND NEW WOODHOUSELEE (OR FULFORD).

The ruins of the original castle of Woodhouselee stand on a bank overlooking the Esk about three miles from the present house, which four or five hundred years ago was the fortalice of

Fulford. Some portions of the ruined walls of old Woodhouselee still remain between Auchendinny and Roslin. Oliver Sinclair, a younger branch of the Rosslyn family, was in possession when, in Queen Mary's time, the estate came into the hands of Belches of Tofts and passed to Couper of Fulford. Under Couper the lands were forfeited; Sir William Purves of Tofts obtained a gift of the estate, and in 1657 procured a charter from Cromwell erecting the lands of Fulford into a barony. It was in Purves's time that stones and material from old Woodhouselee were conveyed to Fulford for a new building. A ghost clung to the stones of its old habitation, and gave several generations as lively a time as has been more recently recorded of the mansion of Ballechin in Strathtay. A portion of the old building remains below the present tower in the form of the vaulted kitchen and the immensely thick walls, which were pierced by a spiral staircase. Purves sold Woodhouselee to his son-in-law James Deans, who was proprietor of the inn in Anchor Close, High Street, where Burns used to carouse. At the end of the seventeenth century his son Robert Deans came into possession. Alexander Pitcairn was the next laird, who in 1735 sold the Mains of Woodhouselee to Patrick Crichton, saddler in Edinburgh. It was Patrick Crichton himself or his son Alexander who sold the place to William Tytler in 1748. Sir Alexander Crichton of this family, born in 1763, was physician-in-ordinary to Alexander I. of Russia, an authority on mental diseases, and advocated the use of vapour of tar in cases of consumption. William Tytler in 1755 pulled down the old tower of Fulford, and the present house was built by his son Lord Woodhouselee in 1796. The south wing was designed and built under the superintendence of G. M. Kemp, architect of the Scott Monument. Several of the later lairds made alterations and improvements.

We give the commonly accepted tradition regarding Woodhouselee. James Hamilton of Bothwellhaugh had been one of Queen Mary's firmest supporters, and fought for her at Langside, where he was made prisoner and sentenced to death. Woodhouselee became the property of Hamilton through his marriage to Lady Anne Sinclair of the Rosslyn family. Regent Moray

spared the life of Bothwellhaugh, but forfeited his estates, which
he gave to his favourite Bellenden, the Justice-Clerk. Bothwellhaugh, thinking that Woodhouselee was not included in the
forfeiture, placed his wife there with her infant child, and went to
join the Earl of Hamilton at Cadzow Castle. Bellenden took the
castle of Woodhouselee in his absence, which he burned to the
ground. Lady Anne was turned out to the woods with her child,
where she went mad, and perished. It is her ghost, with child in
arms, which has haunted old and new Woodhouselee. A considerable part of the present mansion is built from the stones of
the old castle, and the ghost clung to and followed the stones.
Hamilton took vengeance on Regent Moray by shooting him,
from a window in Linlithgow, ere a year had passed. The higher
critics, such as John Hill Burton, have tried to prove that Lady
Anne was alive after the death of Regent Moray, and that the
real ghost was Lady Anne Bothwell, whose lament is well known.
It is said that she and her infant, having been deserted by her
husband, returned to Woodhouselee only in time to die. One or
other of these stories has given the place the reputation of being
haunted. Scott worked the story, as we have said, into his
"Cadzow Castle," where he calls Hamilton's wife Margaret, and
in the "Gray Brother" there is the well-known reference to
"haunted Woodhouselee" and memories of rambles in the neighbourhood :—

> Sweet are the paths, O passing sweet !
>   By Eske's fair streams that run,
> O'er airy steep, through copsewood deep,
>   Impervious to the sun.
>
>   .   .   .   .   .
>
> From that fair dome, where suit is paid
>   By blast of bugle free,
> To Auchendinny's hazel glade,
>   And haunted Woodhouselee.

THE GHOST.

The story goes that in some of the old rooms a mysterious
knocking at the door is heard, a distinct, loud, treble knock,

which sends the servants to answer it. Many visitors have heard the knocking, either in the garden room, the laird's room, the Shepherd's room (so named because Allan Ramsay frequently slept there), or the tower room. Lady Anne was said to pass up the wooden stair which winds between these three last rooms. Once an old coachman, Sutherland by name, and his family, were acting as caretakers of the house in the absence of the family in winter. Sutherland had gone to feed the horses about six o'clock, when his wife and daughter were terrified to hear a loud and reiterated knocking at the hall side-door. The terrier in the side-room heard the sound also, and began barking furiously. Neither mother nor daughter dared rise to go and see who or what was thundering at the door. Woodhouselee stands alone on the hill-side, and they were afraid of tramps or bad characters. The knocking continued at intervals until seven, and the dog kept barking also. When Sutherland returned, they summoned courage to go to the side-door with a lantern. The snow was lying several inches deep, and untrodden ; the avenue, too, was untrodden, which only deepened the mystery of that still, calm night. Again, two ladies were burning nuts at Hallowe'en in the Shepherd's room, which is in the tower, and one of them rose to invite another friend to join them. Just on the instant that she rose, she heard, as she thought, her brother pass the door of the room and go up the little wooden stair. A little later a heavier step passed to the tower room. It was found that no one in the house, known to them, had passed that way. The other experiences have been those of guests awakened by knocking. None of these things has ever been explained. A shooting-tenant of Ballechin, Perthshire, told his servants that the first one who heard any warnings or knocking could go. This threat laid the ghost in the meantime. It seems to be laid here also !

SCOTT AT WOODHOUSELEE.

The great romancer was plain Walter Scott when he haunted Woodhouselee, for he had just set up his household gods in what Miss Tytler thought a poor, dilapidated cottage, with but one good sitting-room, between Lasswade and Loanhead, which may still be seen. On walking over to Scott's cottage at Lasswade one morning, they found him mounted on a ladder nailing together a Gothic arch of willows over the entrance gate. He was very proud of his handiwork, and had gone out to admire it in the moonlight on the first night.

Scott was a frequent visitor at Woodhouselee for days at a time when he started housekeeping at Lasswade. After breakfast he commonly proposed a walk, and, says Miss Ann Fraser Tytler, "with his joyous look and vigorous step, he would take his way towards what was called the Green Hill of Castlelaw. It was rugged of ascent, but the summer wind as it blew upon us came laden with the fragrance of the wild thyme and purple heather, with which it was covered to the very top." They halted at a particular spot, when Scott would start one of his delightful stories, generally the production of his brain at the moment; sometimes he told legends of Covenanters, for there were graves of these men just over Logan Burn at Rullion Green. To these mornings would succeed the evening ghost stories, when the young folks were so excited and spellbound that no one dared move. "How," says Miss Tytler, "could we dare doubt the truth of every word, having ourselves our own legitimate ghost to be believed in?"

At the time of Scott's visits there was one bedroom in the house which, though of no extraordinary dimensions, was always called "the *big* bedroom." Two sides of the walls of this room were covered with very old tapestry, representing subjects from Scripture. Near the head of the bed there was a mysterious-looking, small, and very old door, which led into a turret fitted up as a dressing-room. From this small door the ghost was wont to issue. No servant would enter "the big bedroom after dusk, and even in daylight they went in pairs."

To the old nurse Cicy Low, and her daughter Betty the dairy-maid, Lady Anne had frequently appeared. Old Catherine, when asked about Lady Anne, would say, "'Deed, I have seen her times out o' number, but I am in no ways feared. I ken weel she canna gang beyond her commission; but there's that silly, feckless thing Betty, she met her in the lang passage ae night in the winter-time, and she hadna a drap o' bluid in her face for a fortnight after. She says Lady Anne came sae near her she could see her dress quite weel; it was a Manchester muslin with a wee flower." Walter Scott used to laugh heartily at this "wee flower," and hoped that Lady Anne would never change her dress.

THE HIGHLANDERS HERE DURING THE '45.

It is a shock to come suddenly from these gloaming stories to the matter-of-fact lair or tenant of Woodhouselee, who set down all that he knew and saw of the '45 in Edinburgh and his neighbourhood. The diary begins on that Sabbath of September 15 when the worshippers in Glencorse Church were startled by the news that Prince Charlie and his men were marching on Edinburgh. The long sermon by John Wilson, and an "ill-timed exhortation," were heard with impatience, and the writer hurried to an eminence of the Pentlands from which the dragoons could be seen at Corstorphine. Next day he saw the cavalcade with the baggage and "Highland wifes," as already noted, pass the Braid Hills towards the camp at Duddingston, and caught a glimpse from Canaan Muir, Morningside, of the Prince and his men on their way to Holyrood. He entered the town by the Bristo Port, which, to his indignation, he saw was "in the keeping of these caterpillars; a boy stood with a rusty drawn sword, and two fellows with things like guns of the sixteenth century sat on each side the entry to the Poor House, and these were catching the vermin from the lurking-places about their plaids, and throwing them away." Our friend the laird asked of the Rev. A. W. Jardine, minister of Liberton, "Are these the scoundrels who have surprised Edinburgh by treachery?" The minister replied that he had rather seen the town in the hands of Frenchmen; but the devil and the deep sea are both bad. Then follows a description of the proclamation at the Cross, of the surprise at Prestonpans, and of the whole neighbourhood being overrun by Highlanders on the pretext of searching for arms, which meant the seizing and carrying away, as by Border reivers, of anything that was neither too hot nor too heavy.

They visited Boghall, Glencorse, and Howgate, where they put all Charles Straton's baps and ale on a large fire, and drank whisky. From Woodhouselee they get a little money, and bear away the sheets hidden in the hay; from a terrified serving-man hiding in the garden they extract five shillings and sixpence. They retire behind Woodhouselee, quarrel over the booty, march towards Edinburgh, stop a carriage, and then "gulravage" in the public-house at Lothian Burn. Secretary Murray is seen riding past to Linton, one of his men being mounted on Colonel Gardiner's horse. Lord Maxwell, a son of the Earl of Nithsdale, also rides past. A fellow captured at Castlelaw has on a fur hat and shirt with cambric ruffles down the breast, very clean, and not bleeding. "No doubt he had robbed the shirt," says the writer.

When Prince Charles was appealed to regarding these depredations by men from Swanston and others, he said if the thieves were pointed out they would be hanged. No more came of it; but the Laird of Woodhouselee no doubt heaved a sigh of relief when with his "prospect glass" he had a clear view of the Highland host, with pipes playing, and replenished in horses, goods, and gear, passing on by Milton Bridge to Peebles. "All General Cope's wagons taken at Prestonpans were there. Deserters here and there were picked up; three found on Castlelaw were brought to Woodhouselee; one was wounded by a stone in the head, and all bloody." They were carried forward to Boghall, the next farm, Edinburghwards, and the tables being turned upon them, they were relieved of five guineas and a crown.

The ghost is of such stuff as dreams are made of: here we have the rude and rough reality of the time. It supplements what Dr Carlyle of Inveresk set down in his autobiography, and the notes of Campbell the banker, as published by the Scottish History Society. We may not mention the pictures at Woodhouselee, although some of the Dutch, Italian, and English and Scottish schools are of rare interest. The sword of Claverhouse, which was in his hand when he fell at Killiecrankie, July 16, 1689, is a valuable relic. A former minister of Cockpen, to whom it belonged, had it hung above his bed, and on holidays would take it down, present it solemnly to friends, and make them kiss it. It is a light rapier, with no ornamentation. A small silver medal is attached, with a motto. Then there is Queen Mary's watch and solitaire, given to her French attendant Massie on the eve of her execution. The watch came to the Tytlers through the Rev. Mr Torrance of Glencorse Church, in gratitude to the Woodhouselee family for having presented his father and himself to the living. The watch is a round gold one, perfectly plain, one inch in diameter, made by Hubert in Rouen. The solitaire is set with diamonds, rubies, and pearls, in the centre a tiny figure of a cupid playing with a mouse, and on the reverse is a motto. It is said to have been given to Mary by the Dauphin before their marriage. In a portrait which was in the possession of the second Earl of Buchan she is represented as wearing it. There is a kind of poetical justice in these relics coming here : a Tytler who founded the Scottish branch came over from France in Queen Mary's retinue, and a later member of the family wrote in her defence.

A SUMMERHOUSE.

Sir William Purves of Woodhouselee, whose portrait by Lely is in the Scottish National Portrait Gallery, is said by some to have been the original of Sir William Worthy in Ramsay's "Gentle Shepherd." A "Temple" or rustic summerhouse, on the bank behind the house, has this inscription on its table :—

"Allano Ramsay et genio loci."

" Here midst these scenes that taught thy Doric muse
  Her sweetest song ; the hills, the wood, and stream,
  Where beauteous Peggy strayed, listening the while
  Her Gentle Shepherd's tender tale of love ;
  Scenes which thy pencil, true to nature, gave
  To live for ever, Sacred to this Shrine,
  And unprofaned by ruder hands the stone
  That owes its honour to thy deathless name."

The connection of Allan Ramsay with New Woodhouselee is not very direct !

THE BUSH.

Beyond Woodhouselee is the pretty hamlet of Easter Howgate, smaller than of yore, and said to have suggested Elizabeth Hamilton's "Cottagers of Glenburnie," when the authoress was staying at Woodhouselee. On through a fine avenue of beech trees, we pass the entrance to the Bush, built by Lieutenant-Colonel Robert Archibald Trotter, Postmaster-General for Scotland, at the end of the 18th century, in Italian villa style, and improved in 1843. The family of Trotter was of Berwickshire origin. The lands of Glencorse here, in the seventeenth century, belonged to a family named Bothwell, descended from the Bishop who performed the marriage ceremony between Queen Mary and the Earl of Bothwell. Glencorse House, built about 1812, and Loganbank, below Glencorse House, built about 1810, came into the hands of the Dean of the Faculty of Advocates, afterwards Lord President Inglis, in 1855.

GLENCORSE OLD KIRK.

Window, Glencorse Old Church.

The road to the left at Glencorse Manse leads to Milton Bridge and Fishers' Tryst. In the wood through which winds Glencorse Burn, to the south-east of Rullion Green, are the ruins of the old Church of Glencorse, dating, however, no further back than 1665; having been destroyed by fire in 1695, it was rebuilt in 1699 and enlarged by adding transepts. The ruins no doubt stand on the site of an older building. When the church was repaired in 1811, an ancient font stone was found below the surface of the floor. After it was deserted in 1885 for the handsome new church close by, it was allowed to become a ruin. Glencross was the old name, possibly from a cross in the valley.

MEMORIES OF GLENCORSE BY R. L. STEVENSON.

Stevenson thus refers to Glencorse Burn :—" Do you know," he wrote from Samoa to Mr Crockett, "that the dearest burn to me in the world is that which drums and pours in cunning wimples in that glen of yours behind Glencorse old kirk. Oh that I were the lad I once was, sitting under old Torrance, that old shepherd of let-well-alone, and watching with awe the waving of the old

Glencorse Old Church.

black gloves over the Bible—the preacher's white finger-ends meanwhile aspiring through ! Man, I would even be willing to sit under you—a sore declension, truly—just to be *there*." The Mr Torrance mentioned here left Queen Mary's gold watch to Professor Fraser-Tytler of Woodhouselee, and has his name inscribed on a stone in Glencorse churchyard. There is a fine new church close by. Stevenson thus describes the old church in a note to Sidney Colvin : " It is a little cruciform place, with a steep slate roof. The small kirkyard is full of old gravestones; one of a Frenchman from Dunkerque. I suppose he died prisoner in the military prison hard by; and one, the most pathetic memorial I ever saw, a poor school-slate in a wooden frame, with the inscription cut into it evidently by the father's own hand." It is believed that part of the scenery here is worked into Chapter VI. of "Weir of Hermiston," and it haunted Stevenson to the last. According to the author's mother, Overshiels near Stow also supplied part of the setting. "I shall never," he wrote to Mr Crockett, "take that

Glencorse Reservoir from Turnhouse Hill.

walk by the Fisher's Tryst and Glencorse. I shall never see Auld Reekie. I shall never set my foot again on the heather. . . . Do you know where the road crosses the burn under Glencorse Church? Go there and say a prayer for me. See that it is a sunny day; I would like it to be Sunday; but that's not possible in the premises; and stand on the right bank just where the road goes down into the water, and shut your eyes; and if I don' appear to you!"

STEVENSON'S "PENTLAND RISING."

Stevenson's earliest published effort, at sixteen, was an account of the "Pentland Rising." His mother arranged for its publication with Mr Andrew Elliot, the publisher of this book, at 17 Princes Street (from which shop *Blackwood's Magazine* began its career); it is entitled "The Pentland Rising: a Page of History, 1666," and was anonymous. Mr Gosse in the Pentland edition of Stevenson's Works tells us that it was founded on a novel which the boy had begun, at the age of 15. His father did not think it worthy of continuation, but thought that the author might, in a more sober historical spirit, preserve a record of the rising. It is dated 28th November 1866. One hundred copies were printed of this twenty-two page pamphlet, in bright green cover, at a total cost of about three pounds fifteen shillings. Yet the publisher had afterwards to pay some twelve pounds for one of his own pamphlets when Stevenson became famous. The same feeling for the heather and Covenanting graves breathes in his fine lyric, "Blows the wind to-day," which is reminiscent of Pentland rambles.

RULLION GREEN MARTYRS' MONUMENT.

Between Glencorse Burn and the road is the Preaching Field, where in the month of July an annual service is held on a Sabbath afternoon, in commemoration of the battle of Rullion Green, which was fought on the eastern slope of Turnhouse Hill. The Crawley water cistern (1822) is in the same field. Flotterstone Bridge has been widened in order to carry Talla water pipe.

A monument at Rullion Green bears the following inscriptions:—
"Here and near to this place lyes the Reverend Mr John Crookshanks and Mr Andrew M'Cormock ministers of the Gospel and about

Covenanters' Stone, Rullion Green.

fifty other true covenanted Presbyterians who were killed in this
place in their own inecent self-defence and defence of the
covenanted work of Reformation by Thomas Dalziel of Bins upon
the 28 of November 1666 Rev. 12·11.   Erected Sept. 28, 1738."

On the other side are the following verses :—

> "A cloud of witnesses lyes here,
> Who for Christ's interest did appear,
> For to restore true Liberty
> Overturned then by Tyranny
> And by Proud Prelats who did rage
> Against the Lord's own heritage.
> They sacrificed were for the Laws
> Of Christ their King, his noble cause.
> These heroes fought with great renown,
> By falling got the Martyrs Crown."

An entry in Penicuik Parish Records states that 3s. 4d. was
paid shortly after the battle to the "bellman" for making "west-
landmen's graves."

STORY OF THE RISING OF 1666.

The Rising, which ended in the battle of Rullion Green, had
its beginning in a scuffle at Dalry, in Galloway, with the soldiery.
Sir James Turner had been commissioned by Government to
arrest all who signed the Covenant in the south-west of Scotland.
The Covenanters in that quarter, driven from hearth and home,
took action in defence ; went to Dumfries ; surprised Turner,
taking him prisoner on the 14th November 1666 ; marched
northward to Ayr, where they received as recruit James Wallace,
who had been in the Parliamentary Army in the English Civil
Wars with the rank of colonel.   A bailie of Dumfries reported
this personally to the Privy Council, who instructed Dalziel of
Binns to go westward to Glasgow, and follow the Covenanters.
Hearing of this they went eastward to Lanark, numbering, at that
time, about 1000 men, and then on to Bathgate.   Their motive
for marching, in wretchedly wet and stormy weather, in this direction, was the information that reinforcements would be added to

them at West Calder and Shotts. Reaching Bathgate, they turned towards Edinburgh on the assurance that there they would find friends in their favour, and arrived at Newbridge, near Kirkliston, on the 27th November, going thence to Colinton, where they remained till the morning of the eventful 28th. By this time the forces had fallen to 800 or 900, only partly under arms. Disappointed at not receiving any encouragement from Edinburgh, they resolved to return south to Clyde and Teviotdale, but Dalziel, who had followed them from Lanark to Currie, barred their return through the Pentlands. They therefore, on leaving Colinton, crossed the Braid Burn, passed Dreghorn Castle and Swanston, and, on reaching the Biggar Road, went south in the direction of West Linton. Crossing the Glencorse Burn at Flotterstone, or Ingliston as it was then called, they halted at Rullion Green.

Meanwhile, learning of their movements, Dalziel left Currie and marched along the ravine of Cleuch Maid Stone (see Route No. 4), past St Catherine's Hope, with the view of intercepting them. When his troops came in sight, about noon, the Covenanters left the encampment at Rullion Green, went south under the shelter of the east side of Lawhead Hill, and drew themselves up on the east side of Turnhouse Hill.

Here, to the south-west of where is now the Martyrs' Monument, the battle was fought under the leadership of Wallace, his infantry being in the centre, flanked on the left by the horse under Learmont, and on the right by the horse under Barscobe. The Covenanters numbered 900 horse and foot. Dalziel's forces were variously estimated from 600 horse and 2000 foot, to 3000 foot besides horse.

On the first attack Dalziel was routed. The fight was resumed about sunset, and ended in the defeat and flight of the Covenanters. Turner, who had been with them as prisoner all the time, being now at liberty, rejoined his own party. About 150 were taken prisoners, the rest fled, many of them in the direction of Carlops. Local tradition affirms that some were killed by the Penicuik inhabitants, in the neighbourhood of Coates Farm, a place on the east side of the Biggar Road, and south of the battlefield.   Others going westward were lost in the Pentland bogs, bodies being discovered long after in perfect preservation. General Wallace escaped to Holland, and died there in 1676. The story of a Covenanter's grave near West Linton is given in a later page.

One of the officers in the field against the Covenanters was General Drummond, who wrote the annexed letter giving his account of the battle.   A cadet of the Madertie branch of the family, he supported the Royalist cause both in England, where he was imprisoned after Worcester, and in Scotland as an emissary from Charles II. to the forces under Glencairn. He accompanied Dalziel in the foreign levies of the Czar Michaelovitch, and returned with that officer to Scotland in 1685, and was appointed Major-General of the new Scottish Forces.   One of his earliest duties was to take the field with Dalziel's van against the Covenanters in the south-west.

GENERAL DRUMMOND DESCRIBES THE BATTLE.

"The rebells were at Collintone 2 myles from Edinburgh on Tuesday the 27th by midday to our admiration.   Whatever their designe or invitacon was for so desperate a March they found ther plot p'vented, wee judged rightly they would gett of to Bigger, and ortook us to fall in their way going over the Pentland Hills at Currie.   Our fore party of about 100 horse discovered them on their march towards Linton the Bigger way near a place called Glencors kirk and that spent 2 houres, soe had God blinded these fooles to neglect their advantage, our party being in a ground whence they could not come of.

"Some sharpe charges past in this time which the rebells gave and received with desperate resolution to our prejudice, at last our horse comes on and gave breathing to that weary party but our foot was yet 4 miles from us, wee found it convenient to draw from that ground very advantageous for their foot, wch they after much consideration began to imploy agst us, but wee prevented them & gott of a little to a better ground where they made a fashion to annoy us without any gaine.   Soe soon as our foot came up we put ourselves in order & embattled in a fair plaine upon their noses, they upon the hill above did the like but gave us no disturbance tho' well they might, by this time the sun was sett, wee must make haste and advanced a partie of horse and foot from our right hand to assault their left wing of horse wch instantly came down and met them, & there the work began, wee fought obstinately a long time wth swords untill they mixed like chessmen in a bag, we advanced our right wing and they their left to give reliefe, there again it was disputed toughly. Then came a strong party of foot from their body & forced our right wing back to the foot in some disorder but this was instantly rectified. Their right wing of horse came from their ground foolishly and crosses their foot apprehending their left wing to be in distresse wherein they were mistaken & soe gave their left wing their slack, wch opportunity wee had hold on & there went their cavalrie in disorder. Our whole body then advanced & beat in their horse upon their foot. Then confusion and flight followed. Wee pursued in the dark, killed all the foot & but for the night & steep hills had wholly destroyed them. Some prisoners there are fitt for examples. I know not how many but I conjecture not above 140, for there was sound payment.

"Our losse I cannot tell, but it is greater than many of their skins were worth, their number was about 15 or 1600, & would without doubt have encreased if God had not confounded their imaginacons & rebellious dispositions. Upon Monday the rebells swore the covenant at Lenrick & all to die in defence of it most of these who led their troopes were cashiered preachers.

"Now I trust your grace is at ease. I am.

"Y^r gr^{ces}

"most obedient & most humble serv^t

"W. DRUMMOND."

Endorsed, "Letter from Major Gen^{all} Drummond to the E. of Rothes of the defeat of the rebells in Scotland. 29 Nov. 66. rec. 4th Dec. 1666 in a letter from the Lord Arlington."

HOUSE OF MUIR—MAURICEWOOD.

At House of Muir farm, below Rullion Green, there is a by-path to Glencorse. In 1612 the city of Edinburgh was granted right of holding markets at House of Muir.

Mauricewood, opposite Rullion Green, on the east side of the Biggar road, is where the terrible Mauricewood pit disaster occurred (1889). The pit had caught fire while seventy men and boys were underground.

Return can be made by walking from Flotterstone Bridge, by Glencorse Reservoir, to Colinton, 5¼ miles (Route 3); or train from Glencorse Station, 14½ miles to Waverley Station; or from Penicuik.

Covenanters' Stone, Rullion Green.

CHAPTER IV.

Route 2.

FROM MERCHISTON BY CRAIGLOCKHART TO DREGHORN AND COLINTON.

Merchiston Castle—Meggetland—Craiglockhart—Estate of Craiglockhart—Redhall, Slateford—Colinton House—Story of Lord Dunfermline—Mrs Oliphant's "Open Door"—Colinton Church—Hailes—R. L. Stevenson and Dr Balfour—Old Church Discipline—Notable Residents—Redford—Dreghorn Castle—Dreghorn Lodge—The Reindeer Cave—Traces of Cromwell near Colinton—Field Paths to Morningside.

MERCHISTON CASTLE—MEGGETLAND.

COLINTON, $4\frac{1}{4}$ miles from the G.P.O., is a good centre for various Pentland rambles. The Gilmore Place tramcar drops one opposite Craiglockhart skating pond ; the Suburban train of North British Railway at Craiglockhart Station ; the Caledonian train at Colinton itself. In walking, should we start from the car-line near Christ Church, Morningside, we skirt the pleasant and healthy suburb of Merchiston, and peep in passing at Merchiston Castle, which was acquired by the family of Napier in 1438. John Napier, the inventor of logarithms, was born here in 1550, and was credited with magical powers ; when the laird of Roslin's pigeons made free with his seed corn, he made them tipsy with grain steeped in some preparation and caught them easily ; he tried to get gold in the Pentlands, and made a contract with Logan of Restalrig regarding the discovery of hidden treasure in Fast Castle.

Where the Union Canal comes close to the road, in a field to the right is a solitary gate-pillar standing in a field. This, with an old pillar sun-dial in the grounds to the left, are all that remains of the mansion of Meggetland, which in the early 18th century belonged to the Sievewrights. The lands on the east side of Craig Hill belonged to a person of the same name.

CRAIGLOCKHART.

Although Scott has not thrown the glamour of his genius over Craiglockhart Hill, as he has done over Blackford, the former, nevertheless, has great variety of outline, with fine woods and

ROUTE NO. 2.

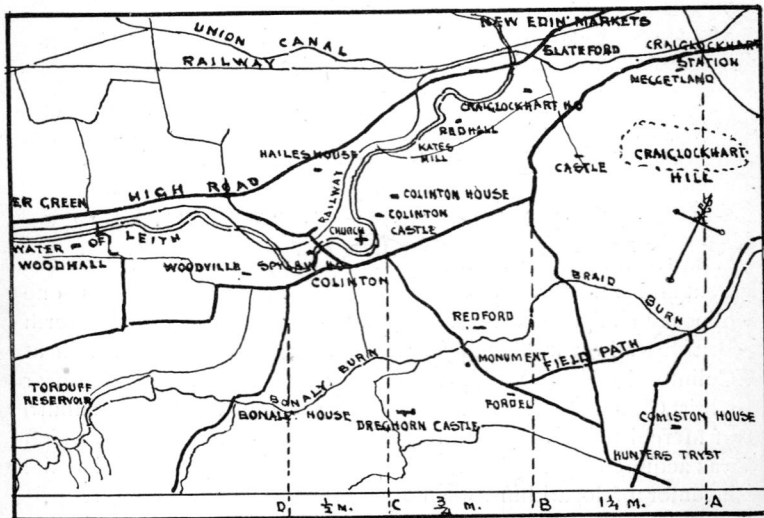

greenery to the north and east to add to its attractions. On a beautiful summer day it offers the perfection of a rural retreat, within easy access of the heart of the city. The eye is gladdened and satisfied from every side, while towards the south hollow of the hill, with the city hid by the mass of Craiglockhart east and west, the pedestrian might imagine himself in a nook of the Highlands. It has not yet been thrown open to the public.

Craig-Hill, or Easter Craiglockhart Hill, and the western hill, now a golf course, are fine specimens of basaltic rock, studded with minerals for the prying geologist. On a lovely day the north face of Easter Craiglockhart, either viewed from the Colinton Road, or overlooked from the summit, affords such a refreshment to the lover of green and quiet places as may be sought for in vain in a long railway journey. In spring the hillside is jubilant with bird music; in summer comes the varied greenery; in autumn the dying tints. In 1838 the kestrel hawk was breeding in the rocks of Craiglockhart; and the precipitous north-east face of the west hill, at the back of the Hydropathic, affords a secure nesting place for the pilfering jackdaw.

There is evidence by Sir Simon Lockhart, from whose family the estate takes its name, of having purchased it from William Lamberton, its previous possessor, about the middle of the thirteenth century. The narrow square tower to the east of the Hydropathic is believed to have been erected by the Lockharts, in the beginning of the sixteenth century. The arched basement storey and the shattered walls of the second storey still remain; but every vestige of the surrounding buildings has disappeared. The estate passed out of the hands of the Lockhart family, but again returned to them. In a paragraph from "Acts of the Scottish Parliament," quoted in the "Statistical Account," we read— "Craig Lockhart—1630, 17th February. The lands of Craig Lockhart were by Act of Parliament disjoined from the parish of West Kirk, and added to the parish of Hailes (Colinton). Sir John Gilmour, of Craigmillar, president of the College of Justice, ratified in the lands of Craig Lockhart, with the tour, fortalice, manor place, &c." Foulis of Colinton, an ancient family in the parish, and at one time the largest landowners, also held Craiglockhart.

ESTATE OF CRAIGLOCKHART.

Sir John Gilmour of Craigmillar purchased the estate of Craiglockhart from the Foulis family, and Sir George Lockhart of Carnwath, also a Lord President, bought back the property into his family. His brother, Sir William Lockhart, married a niece of Oliver Cromwell, and held high office under the Protector. The eldest son of Lord President Lockhart, George Lockhart of Carnwath, was a Jacobite, followed the Pretender, suffered imprisonment, fled to the Continent, but managed to save his estate. He was married to a daughter of the ninth Earl of Eglinton, and was killed in a duel in 1732. His "Memoirs concerning the affairs of Scotland" appeared in 1714 without his knowledge, and the "Lockhart Papers" in 1817. Lockhart had been served heir to his father in Craiglockhart in 1690. He did not hold the place long, but sold it to George Porteous, herald painter to the King. It was sold by a son of the latter, before 1730, to John Parkhill; his son, Captain Parkhill, disposed of it to Dr Monro, only less famous than his celebrated father, Professor of Medicine, Anatomy, and Surgery, in 1779. Although he had no residence on these lands, we are told that Dr Monro took some pleasure in adorning them. He was succeeded by his son, the third doctor of the line, from whom it passed in 1859 to Captain Alexander Monro of Craiglockhart. Its recent history since passing into the hands of the Parochial Board and the Craiglockhart Estate Company, with the erection of Hydropathic, will be familiar to most.

REDHALL—SLATEFORD.

Passing the Reservoir of the Edinburgh Water Trust just beyond the Hydropathic, we go through a fine avenue of trees; to the left is part of the Pentland range beginning at Hillend, and extending westward by Caerketton, Allermuir, Cape Law, and on to White Hill above Bonaly. Redford House is in the hollow below, and Dreghorn Castle Tower shews itself in the woods above on one of the hill spurs. On the right, unseen, lies Slateford—spelt Sclateford at one time according to the inscription on the old collection plates at the U.F. Church, and notable as the birthplace of John Mac Whirter, R.A. Prince Charles Edward, in the '45, slept at Gray's Mill here, before his entry into Edinburgh. Just to the north o Slateford Station is the site of the new Edinburgh Markets an Slaughter Houses, one of the excellent city improvements. Ove the Water of Leith at Gorgie is the site of the Edinburg Exhibition of 1908, in Saughton Park.

South from Slateford is Redhall, the history of which goes back to 1375, when the barony of Redhall, with the exception of the lands of Dreghorn and Woodhall, was conveyed to Robert, son of Robert II., who afterwards became Duke of Albany. It passed in the sixteenth century to Sir Adam Otterburn, whose arms—an otter's head, a crest, and two wyverns for supporters—appear in the old pigeon house. In 1650 it was besieged by Cromwell and ruined in the siege, which lasted a week. It was of importance, as it blocked the way for probable supplies at Queensferry. Leslie's men lay on the slopes of Corstorphine Hill. About a century later the stones of Redhall were used to build the present house and offices. In 1672 the notorious John Chiesley of Dalry was the owner, and in 1755 it went to Mr Inglis, who had in his office for a time Henry Mackenzie, who afterwards wrote "The Man of Feeling." Mr David Chalmers, a nephew of Dr Chalmers, when occupier, did much to disclose the ruins of the old castle.

COLINTON HOUSE.

Colinton Castle lies to the south-west of Redhall, not many yards from Colinton Road. It was attacked and destroyed by Cromwell at the same time as Redhall. After the Restoration the proprietor was created Lord Colinton, and his son raised to the Bench during his father's lifetime, taking the title of Lord Redford.

A small part of the Colinton Estate, including the site of the old Castle, was bought towards the end of the eighteenth century by Sir William Forbes of Pitsligo, who built there Colinton House, which is now in possession of the family of Trotter. Sir William Forbes' grandson, James David Forbes, who shares with Professor Tyndall the honour connected with glacial research in the Alps, got his first information about ice action in the bed of the Water of Leith at Colinton.

STORY OF LORD DUNFERMLINE.

When James, first Lord Dunfermline, third son of General Sir Ralph Abercromby, lived in Colinton House, he was for many years visited twice a week by Dr John Brown, author of "Rab and His Friends." Lord Dunfermline, while gruff in manner, was full of courage, sincerity, and practical sagacity. He gave a letter to Lady Dunfermline one day, in which he said, "Dr Brown has told me I may die suddenly, and therefore there may be no time for parting words, and besides, this would be painful for us both." He then mentioned what she had been to him during their union, "You have been my comfort and my strength all my life." Lady Dunfermline was a sister of the Earl of Minto and of Lady Russell, "a most excellent, sweet, and wise-hearted woman."

MRS OLIPHANT'S "OPEN DOOR."

Mrs Oliphant found a setting here, in the ruins of the manor-house of the Foulises, for one of her "Stories of the Seen and Unseen," called "The Open Door." Here is her description of Colinton :—" Brentwood (Colinton House) stands on that fine and wealthy slope of country, one of the richest in Scotland, which lies between the Pentland Hills and the Firth. In clear weather you could see the blue gleam—like a bent bow, embracing the wealthy fields and scattered houses—of the great estuary on one side of you, and on the other the blue heights, not gigantic like those we had been used to, but just high enough for all the glories of the atmosphere, the play of clouds, and sweet reflections, which gives to a hilly country an interest and a charm which nothing else can emulate. Edinburgh with its two lesser heights—the Castle and the Calton Hill—its spires and towers piercing through the smoke, and Arthur's Seat, lying crouched behind, like a guardian no longer very needful, taking his repose beside the well-beloved charge, which is now, so to speak, able to take care of itself without him—lay at our right hand. From the lawn and drawing-room windows we could see all these varieties of landscape."

The village of "Brentwood"—or Colinton—comes in for a slight descriptive sketch, lying almost under the house, on the other side of the deep little ravine, down which ran a stream which ought to have been lovely and frolicsome, but which had been sacrificed to trade and was grimy with paper-making. That side of the dell was clothed with fine trees; the village lay in the hollow, and climbed, with prosaic houses, the other side. The glen or dell was beautiful at all seasons, and the writer did not dislike the interior of the old-fashioned pewed and galleried church, which has been rebuilt. In the park which surrounded the house were the ruins of the former mansion of Brentwood, which the novelist makes, as it is in reality, much smaller and less important than the solid Georgian edifice which she inhabited. The old building had the remains of a tower, an indistinguishable mass of mason-work, overgrown with ivy. The ruins are further described with a doorway open and vacant, free to all the winds, to the rabbits and every wild creature. "A door that led to nothing—closed once, perhaps, with anxious care, bolted and guarded, now void of any meaning. It impressed me, I remember, from the first." Round the ruin, a pretty domestic story, with its mystery, is cunningly woven: a story which is rationally explained at last, and which we need not spoil by trying to repeat for those who have once read or may still have the pleasure of doing so.

There are some remarkable holly hedges at Colinton Castle, more than forty feet high, referred to by Mr Joseph Sabine in 1827 as supposed to have been planted between 1670 and 1680. Lord Cockburn thought the cedars in the old-fashioned garden very fine.

COLINTON CHURCH—HAILES.

The ancient Church of Colinton, dedicated to St Cuthbert, and founded about the year 1095, is supposed to have stood on the site of Hailes House, which lies on a plateau to the north-east. This house dates from the end of the eighteenth century, and is surrounded by fine well-grown trees. To the south-east the ground slopes towards Colinton Dell, in the Water of Leith valley. There is a well-tower (disused) and some ruins which lend colour to the statement that Hailes or Colinton Church was once situated there, and that it was the site of a monastery. It is said that the Duke of Somerset's invasion of 1544-45 destroyed Hailes Church. Hailes was once inhabited by Samuel Anderson, banker, who left a small endowment to the poor of Colinton parish. Here lived and died Webb Seymour (1855), brother of the Duke of Somerset, who is buried at Holyrood. To the north once stood Easter Hailes, residence of George Drummond, six times Lord Provost of Edinburgh, who founded the Royal Infirmary, and began that series of city improvements of which the end is not yet.

Hailes Quarry, in the vicinity, when the building boom was in progress in Edinburgh from 1820 to 1826, yielded a fortune to its proprietor.

The church was gifted at the beginning of the 12th century by Ethelred, Earl of Fife, second son of Malcolm Canmore, to Dunfermline Abbey; later it belonged to the Preceptory of St Anthony at Leith. The old church disappeared about 1560. Another site was chosen lower down on a bend of the Water of Leith, and a big timber structure built, but so poorly put together that it fell into ruin about the year 1770. The next church was erected in 1771, and has given place to the present handsome new structure (built in 1907-8), which stands to the north of the bridge crossing the Water of Leith, which was built in 1686. Dr Balfour, minister from 1823 to 1860, is the centre of much of its interest, partly on his own account and also for the sake of his grandson R. L. Stevenson, who often found a home in the manse there.

R. L. STEVENSON AND DR BALFOUR.

In "Memories and Portraits," Stevenson has given a beautiful picture of the old manse as it then was, and of his venerable grandfather: "It was a place in that time like no other," he writes; "the garden cut into provinces by a great hedge of beech, and overlooked by the church and the terrace of the churchyard, where the tombstones were thick; flower-plots lying warm in the sunshine. . . . The smell of water rising all round, with an added tang of paper mills; the sound of water everywhere, and the sound of mills—the wheel and the dam singing their alternate strains; the birds on every bush and from every corner of the overhanging woods pealing out their notes until the air throbbed with them; and in the midst of this, the manse."

"I read him," writes Stevenson of Dr Balfour, "as a man of singular simplicity of nature; unemotional, and hating the display of what he felt; a lover of his life and innocent habits to the end. We children admired him; partly for his beautiful face and silver hair, for none more than children are concerned for beauty and, above all, for beauty in the old; partly for the solemn light in which we observed him once a week, the observed of all observers in the pulpit." Into the room where the old man sat in the midst of a library of "bloodless books," the little boy was sent by his mother to repeat a psalm. It was that lyric which no Scotsman hears sung away from home without a moisture in his eyes and a lump in his throat—"I to the hills will lift mine eyes." This is how the man records the childish experience :—

"I went in quaking with fear. . . .

> ' Thy foot He'll not let slide, nor will
> He slumber that thee keeps,'

it ran—a strange conglomerate of the unpronounceable, a sad model to set in childhood before one who was himself to be a versifier, and a task in recitation which merited reward. And I must suppose the old man thought so too, for he took me in his arms and kissed me, and gave me a little kindly sermon for my psalm; so that for that day we were clerk and parson."

OLD CHURCH DISCIPLINE.

During the time of the first church, strict discipline was exercised on the Sabbath-breaker and the intemperate, who had to submit to public rebuke and even to the embrace of the "jougs" and clothing in sackcloth. The absence of fixed pews must have been very disconcerting, each hearer bringing his or her own stool. Thus we read that on 18th November 1774 :—"Isabel Colquhoun being summoned to this dyet, and compearing, was charged with disturbing the neighbours about her in time of sermon. To which the said Isabel answered that she, being the oldest possessor of a chair in the body of the kirk, she thought that the neighbours in Bonally should have more respect to her than toss her chair up and down the kirk as they often did, and that all the noise she made was to get her chair where it had stood three score of years, but that she was sorry for any offence she had given "—whereupon she was "rebuikit" by the kirk session.

The oldest tombstone in the churchyard is thus inscribed, " Here lyes ane Honourable Woman A. Heriot Spous to J Foulis of Collingtoun quha died 8 August 1593," and a massive coffin-shaped iron case used to lie near the gate, a relic of "resurrectionist" days.

NOTABLE RESIDENTS.

While resident at Colinton Bank, Dr Thomas Murray, author of "The Literary History of Galloway," published his very interesting "Biographical Annals of the Parish of Colinton" in 1863. Dr Murray, before his death at Elm Bank, Lasswade, in 1872, had been a pioneer in many important departments of life, and in the successful printing firm now known as Morrison & Gibb. He was a friend and correspondent of Thomas Carlyle and Alexander Murray. He wrote lives of Samuel Rutherford, Leighton, and Wycliffe, and was one of the founders of the Edinburgh Galloway Association in 1843; as also of the Philosophical Institution in 1846. For thirty years he was secretary of the Edinburgh School of Arts. Dr Pryde calls him the autocrat of that school in its formative period—the presiding genius of the place. He had unfailing tact, and never made an enemy. He had written for Sir David Brewster's "Edinburgh Encyclopædia," as his friend Carlyle had also done.

Other notable residents have been Henry Mackenzie and Dr Alison, Professor of the Theory and Practice of Physic in the Edinburgh University, son of Rev. Mr Alison, who died at Woodville, author of the "Essay on the Nature and Principles of Taste," and father of Sir Archibald Alison, the author of the "History of Europe from the French Revolution."

James Ballantine describes Colinton in his "Miller of Deanhaugh," with "its romantic valley, its lines of cottages embedded in the hollows; its kail yairds, and their rows of currant bushes; its sylvan pathways threading the masses of wood, deep, deep down in the beautiful Dell." The Dell is indeed lovely, and is much resorted to by picnic parties in summer-time, who give that touch of homeliness and companionship which always pleasantly relieves the solitude of nature. The stream, at one time foul by discharges from the paper and other mills, is now clean from its source to its outlet—thanks to a drainage scheme.

There also are seen, at the eastern end of Colinton Dell, the ruins of Kate's Mill, where, at one time, it is said, the paper was made on which the Bank of Scotland's first notes were printed.

Westward of the Church, on the left bank of the Water of Leith, was the estate of Spylaw, which belonged to James Gillespie, who realised, by the manufacture of tobacco and snuff, the fortune which he left for the erection of the Hospital that bears his name at Bruntsfield. His old shop is still to be seen, with a medallion portrait of him upon it, on the north side of the High Street of Edinburgh.

Amongst the modern charitable institutions located at Colinton are the Sir William Fraser Homes for Decayed Authors and Artists; the late Miss Guthrie Wright's Nursing Home; and the Homes for Aged Christians. Colinton and Juniper Green have been growing of late; and fine views of both can be had from Torphin Hill, the red roofs standing out well against the green.

Redford, on Redford Estate, to the south, opposite to Dreghorn, sold in 1906 to the Heriot Trust for £16,000, gave a title in 1674 to a Lord of Session, Sir James Foulis, son of Sir James Foulis, Lord Justice-Clerk. John Allen, who afterwards became an able writer and lecturer on Physiology, and on political and historical subjects, was born at Redford in 1771. He became physician to Lord Holland and his family in 1802, living at Holland House till his death in 1843. He was appointed Master of Dulwich College in 1818. Steeped in the history and traditions of the Whig politicians of the eighteenth century, he was a valued contributor to the *Edinburgh Review*. Lord Macaulay designated him "a man of vast information and great conversational power"; while Lord Byron thought him "the best informed and one of the ablest men he knew." His great book was an "Enquiry into the Rise and Growth of the Royal Prerogative," while he also published a " Vindication of the Ancient Independence of Scotland."

DREGHORN CASTLE.

Dreghorn Castle was begun in the seventeenth century by Sir William Murray, Master of the Works to Charles II. Marrying the daughter of Sir James Foulis of Colinton, he came into possession of the property. The Pitcairns of Dreghorn are derived from Principal Alexander Pitcairn of St Andrews, grandson of the sixteenth Pitcairn of that Ilk ; and, as a well-known inscription in Colinton churchyard records, from this branch were descended, among a host of other distinguished persons, Dr Robertson, the historian, and Lord Brougham. Mr George Home of Kelloe became the owner in 1720, into whose family a tutor entered, David Malloch, or Mallet, the author of "William and Margaret," the famous ballad composed by him as he wandered on the banks of the Redford or Braid Burn. He was tutor to Home's sons from 1720 to 1723.

The Rev. Adam Gib, leader of the Anti-Burghers, who were the last to deliver up their arms to Prince Charlie's men, in 1745, assembled his flock at Dreghorn, and lifted up his testimony every Sunday against "an unnatural and un-Christian rebellion headed by a Popish Pretender." There was usually a party of the rebel guard from Colinton standing about watching developments.

About 1762, John Maclaurin, son of Professor Maclaurin of the Mathematical Chair in Edinburgh University, bought the property with the proceeds of the sale of his paternal estate of Drygrange, in Roxburghshire. He was a Member of the Faculty of Advocates, and being raised to the Bench in the year 1788, assumed the title of Lord Maclaurin.

Lord Maclaurin is said to have at this time added a storey to the old manor-house. His eldest son, Colin Maclaurin, sold the estate within a year of his father's death to Mr Alexander Trotter of the " Bush " family. It came, in 1862, by purchase, into the hands of Mr R. A. Macfie, some time M.P. for the

Leith Burghs, who erected several monuments in the vicinity, one in front of the gamekeeper's house further east in memory of General Gordon, and others nearer his own entrance to the Covenanters, close to the conjoined four columns, which, with the façade adjoining the Redford gate, were part of the old Edinburgh Infirmary front, designed by the elder Adam. It contains the names of persons associated with the history of the district.

AT DREGHORN LODGE.

Before leaving Redford, the visitor will do well to rest on the picturesque bridge parapet, and confirm any pleasant impressions he may have received from the beauty of the neighbourhood. The bridge spans the Redford or Braid Burn. Fine examples of firs and beech are all around, rising out of dense underwood, from which the rhododendrons blaze out in colour in due season. Snowberry there is also, and a wealth of primroses in their time. The place is a paradise for singing birds, the cuckoo being heard in its season, and the stream is rippled and circled by the movements of water hens, which rest there. A little further away is a group of lime trees, fresh in their delicate green foliage, and humming with insect life on a warm summer day. If consent is gained, the pedestrian may pass through the gate opposite the lodge, and walk for a mile on the paved way beside the burn, emerging near the Colinton Road. The Braid Burn, according to Mr Tom Speedy, is the haunt of the heron, the kingfisher, and the wild duck in one part or another of its course, and he reports having on one occasion seen an otter in that part of it which runs through Duddingston Park.

THE REINDEER CAVE.

To the south of Dreghorn Mains, near the foot of what is called the hundred steps, which ascend the hills on the Dreghorn estate, a cave was found, by Mr R. A. Macfie, in 1886. Papers were read a good many years ago at a meeting of the Edinburgh Geological Society by Mr John Henderson and Mr James Simpson, of the Anatomical Museum of Edinburgh University : " On mammalian remains discovered in a rock fissure on the face of the Green Crag, Pentland Hills, on the estate of Dreghorn." Mr Simpson said the remains contained bones of the horse, wolf, and fox, but the greater number were those of the reindeer, and represented parts of at least five individuals of that species. The condition of the bones and their environment seemed to show that they constituted part of the contents of the lair of some large carnivora, for they were gnawed and split up in the manner characteristic of the bones of the prey of such carnivora as the hyena. Mr Henderson, in his paper, explained that the rock fissure where the bones were found was cut out of a vein containing a large percentage of lime, and some of the bones, along with fragments of rocks, were cemented together with lime. Others lay loose among the weathered rock that filled the fissure. The fissure was not like a rut cut out by water from the hill, but resembled the well-known fissure at Salisbury Crags termed the "Cat Nick." He thought the fissure had been cut in the rock after the ice of the glacial period had left the district, and when little or no vegetation existed on the hill, and that the carnivorous animals had taken possession before the refilling process had long commenced, as all the bones occupied a position near the bottom. A great time had elapsed and a great change had taken place in the climate since those reindeer bones were dragged into the fissure. It was remarked that the finding of these bones was by far the most important discovery yet made as to the existence of reindeer in Scotland. There is nothing now to be seen on the spot save the rift in the hill.

There is no right of way to the Reindeer Cave; on the opposite side of the Howden Burn is the Green Craig cistern of the Water Trust. From this point eastwards there is a pleasant path along the side of the hills to Swanston.

TRACES OF CROMWELL NEAR COLINTON.

On 13th August 1650, Cromwell left his position at Musselburgh and led his army "towards Colintoun," and wrote to Leslie next day "from the Camp at Pentland Hills," which was on Galachlaw, south of the Braids. On the 27th of the month he tried to engage the Scots army, which had issued "fourth of their trenches, and marched after them towards Corstorphine." An observer has written, "The Scots army being put in some readynes, marched up to Corstorphin Hill, but because the English feared it was too near the Castle of Edinburgh, they would not hazard battail there : wherefore both armies marched to Gogar, Tuesday 27, and played each upon other with their great guns ; but because of Gogar burn, and other ditches betwixt the armies, they could not join battail. Next day, about mid-day, the English began to retire, and went first to their leagar at Braidshill." Cromwell acknowledged 20 killed and wounded, and the enemy 80. The marshy nature of the land may be judged when, even in 1725, two lochs are shown in a contemporary map, one on either side of Corstorphine Kirk. The field at Gogar where Cromwell met with a repulse is now occupied by the houses and grounds of Gogar Burn and Hanley. In the summer of 1651, Cromwell and his Ironsides were again stationed "towards Colingtoun," on Pentland Hills (our old quarters). Colonel Lilburne wrote to Cromwell that the soldiers "eate biskett and cheese on Pentland hills." Old Redhall House had memories of the stout siege when the laird held out, as we have said, against Cromwell, who so admired his powers that he let him go free.

FIELD PATHS TO MORNINGSIDE.

The next route from Colinton may be followed, or a return may be made from Dreghorn by Hunter's Tryst and Fairmilehead to Morningside ; by either of the delightful field paths from Fordel by Oxgangs, or by Comiston Farm. The view of Edinburgh from beyond Fordel, with the Braids and Arthur's Seat in front, would have afforded a fine subject for the brush of Turner.

CHAPTER V.

Route 3.

Popularity of this Route—Bonaly House described—Lord Cockburn on Bonaly—View from Bonaly Tower—A Meeting of the Faithful at Bonaly—Professor Blackie and James Ballantine on Bonaly Burn—A Pawky Pentland Shepherd—Lord Cockburn's Fruitful Suggestion—Hugh Miller on Glencorse—Story of the Hunt of Pentland—Edinburgh Water Supply—St Katherine's Chapel—Gladhouse and Talla.

THIS Colinton to Glencorse by Bonaly route, being so accessible from town, is one of the most popular walks on the Pentlands, although the barbed wire fence on the first half of the hill has taken the sense of freedom from many a pedestrian. The return can be made in many ways—to Currie, by Loganlee to Balerno, or by the old Biggar road and Hillend to Morningside.

BONALY HOUSE.

Red-roofed villas are here creeping up to the foot of the hills. There appears to have been a village of Bonaly to the west of Bonaly House in the year 1652. There were waulk-mills worked by the water power of Bonaly Burn, a distillery, skinnery, and magnesia manufactory, and dwelling houses, of course, but they have all disappeared. Originally a farmhouse, Lord Cockburn altered it in 1845, and since that time it has had further additions. making it the imposing building we now see. There is an excellent description of the place, its outlook, and the approach to it, in Meiklejohn's Life of Professor Hodgson, who lived there from 1874 to 1880. We give Meiklejohn's account here :—

ROUTE NO. 3.

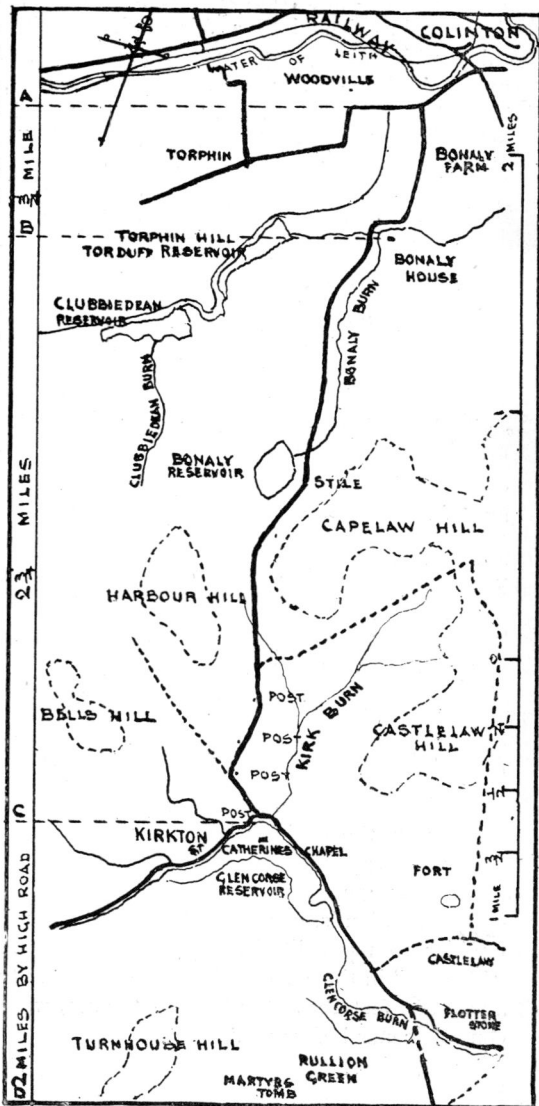

"Striking south for the Pentlands, right for the heart of the lovely hills, he finds the road constantly rising, and the view at every step becomes wider. Suddenly, at its highest point, the road dips again, and before him appears a round tower rising out of a thick mass of trees, and flanked on the right by crags and steeply escarped hills, and where the eye turns to the left, far away across the southern suburbs of Edinburgh, stands the lion form of Arthur's Seat, with the Crags of Salisbury stretching from its base. Turning and looking North, he sees the noble sea-breadth of the Firth of Forth, and the rich shores of the ancient 'Kingdom of Fife.' This ground on which

Bonaly Tower stands seems only a narrow nook, but as you go down, it broadens into a fair garden and broad-spread grounds, thick with beeches, sycamores, pines, and evergreens; a clear mountain burn rushing through the grounds, and the song of birds in every corner. Massive hills shut in the garden from cold and boisterous winds, and a long winding path edged with flower-beds, running along the stream, leads you to the grassy sides of the main range of the Pentland Hills.

LORD COCKBURN ON BONALY.

"Bonaly Tower is a singularly picturesque building, exhibiting the charming variety of round and square outlines, hanging turrets and conical roofs, which belong to the Scotch castellated style. It owes its existence to Lord Cockburn, by whom it is thus described in his 'Memorials.' 'In March 1811 I married, and set up my rural household gods at Bonaly, in the parish of Colinton, close by the northern base of the Pentland Hills; and unless some avenging angel shall expel me, I shall never leave that paradise. I began by an annual lease of a few square yards and a scarcely habitable farm house. But realising the profanations of Auburn, I have destroyed a village and erected a tower, and reached the dignity of a twenty-acred land. Everything except the two burns, the few old trees, and the mountains, is my own work, and to a great extent the work of my own hands. Human nature is incapable of enjoying more happiness than has been my lot here, where the glories of the prospects, and the luxury of the wild retirement, have been all enhanced by the progress of my improvements, of my children, and of myself. I have been too happy, and often tremble in the anticipation that the cloud must come at last. Warburton says there was not a bush in his garden on which he had not hung a speculation. There is not a recess in the valleys of the Pentlands, nor an eminence on their summits, that is not familiar to my solitude. One summer I read every word of "Tacitus" in the sheltered crevice of a rock (called "My Seat"), about 800 feet above the level of the sea, with the most magnificent of scenes before me.'

"The principal entrance of the house is in the round tower, out of which opens a wide spiral staircase, well lit at every stage, which serves as a gallery of engravings and works of art. The dining room, billiard room, and library are on the first floor, a spacious drawing room on the second, with a corridor leading to many bedrooms and quaint nooks ; above are other rooms, while the kitchen and offices occupy the basement. The windows on the south side command a view of soft sunlit lawns and umbrageous sycamores, nestling under the protection of a grand rounded recess of the Pentlands, which rise 1000 feet above the sea level, and 500 above the ground floor of the house. Passing from gardens fit for 'learned leisure,' the visitor finds a great choice of walks—some straight, some winding through variegated shrubberies, and others leading through wild woods up the mountain, or beside the sparkling burn, sometimes murmuring a quiet tune, and at others gushing down its miniature waterfalls, and in winter often overflowing its banks. On the north side of the house the views are of wider range, stretching over cornfields and across the Firth to the wooded shores of Fife.

VIEW FROM BONALY TOWER.

" If we go to the top of the tower, and out upon the roof of the main building, we shall have before us a view such as is seldom to be seen, even in Scotland. The eye has a range of at least eighty miles, and takes in highlands and lowlands, town and country. The distant peaks of the Perthshire Grampians ; the higher mountains of the Trossachs, Ben Ledi, Ben Lomond, Ben Aan ; the green rounded masses of the Ochils ; the level valley of the winding Forth ; the escarpment of the table-land of Kinross ; the twin Lomonds of Fife ; nearer the gentle wooded heights of Corstorphine ; the mighty belt of the great sea-river ; the solitary Arthur's Seat ; the conical Berwick Law ; the stumpy mass of the Bass Rock ; the regular streets of Edinburgh, broken into by the rugged hump of Craiglockhart—all this and more the eye takes in with ease and delight. There are few landscapes more beautiful or more varied. Eight counties—Perthshire, Stirlingshire, Clackmannan, Kinross, Fife, the three Lothians—fall into it.

"Walk through the grounds, up by the side of the clear burn—clear and bright as a cut Scotch pebble—pass out by a little wicket-gate, and you come at once on the green hillsides, where for miles and miles no human being or house or sign of habitation can be seen, and where the mountain silence is broken by the scream of the lapwing, or the bleating of the dotted sh."

After Lord Cockburn's death, Bonaly was purchased by an Gray of the *North British Advertiser*. Other proprietors have been William T. Thomson, Hodgson, and Simpson.

A MEETING OF THE FAITHFUL AT BONALY.

There was in existence in 1842 a "Bonaly Friday Club," with three dozen members, many of them afterwards known to fame, who enjoyed themselves here.

Lord Cockburn, in the autumn of 1853, invited James Nasmyth, of steam-hammer fame, to have a "hill day" at Bonaly, and to bring "the faithful" with him. These included his wife, David Roberts, Clarkson Stanfield, Louis and Carl Haag, Sir George Harvey, James Ballantine, and D. O. Hill, all artists. "We made our way," writes Nasmyth, "to bonny Bonaly, a charming residence, situated at the foot of the Pentland Hills. The day was perfect, in all respects 'equal to bespoke.' With that most genial of men, Lord Cockburn, for our guide, we wandered far up the Pentland Hills. After a rather toilsome walk, we reached a favourite spot. It was a semi-circular hollow in the hillside, scooped out by the sheep for shelter. It was carpeted and cushioned with a deep bed of wild thyme, redolent of the very essence of rural fragrance. We sat down in a semi-circle, our guide in the middle. He said in his quaint, peculiar way, 'Here endeth the first lesson.' After gathering our breath, and settling ourselves to enjoy our well-earned rest, we sat in silence for a time. The gentle breeze blew past us, and we inhaled the fragrant air. It was enough for a time to look on, for the glorious old city was before us, with its towers, and spires, and lofty buildings between us and the distance. On one side Arthur's Seat, and on the other the Castle, the crown of the city. The view extended far and wide on to the waters of the Forth, and the blue hills of Fife. The view is splendidly described by David Macbeth Moir : "

> " Traced like a map, the landscape lies
> In cultured beauty, stretching wide :
> Here Pentland's green acclivities,
> There ocean, with its swelling tide,
> There Arthur's Seat, and, gleaming through
> Thy southern wing, Dun Edin blue !
> While in the Orient, Lammer's daughters,
> A distant giant range, are seen ;
> North Berwick Law with cone of green,
> And Bass amid the waters."

There was haggis on the bill of fare at Bonaly that day, and the host, master in the art of conversation, was quick, ready, and full of wit.

PROFESSOR BLACKIE AND BONALY BURN.

Professor Blackie, poet and scholar, wrote the following lines on the mountain burn which runs through the grounds. The wise thinker was Professor Hodgson :—

THE BURN O' BONALY.

> " 'Twas a cold gleamy day, all hueless and grey,
> When the keen March winds whistled over the brae,
>   That I wandered alone up the valley,
> Behind the old tower where the wise thinker dwells,
> 'Neath the smooth grassy brae, and the clear-flowing wells
>   Of the bonnie green burn o' Bonaly.

> " I wound me alone up the cleft of the brae,
> O'er the wreck of the winter a wild rocky way,
>   By the bonnie green burn o' Bonaly ;
> Long patches of snow on the brown heather ay,
> And a voice on the sough of the blast seemed to say,
>   From the bonnie green burn o' Bonaly, —

> " What seekest thou here in a time without cheer,
> When the braes are all bare, and the hills are all drear,
>   Thou foolish old wandering rhymer,
> When the lone glen pipes with the shriek of the storm,
> And no chaunt of the light plumy people to charm
>   The ear of the mountain climber?

E

"Go, get thee to town, and stow thee away,
All snugly and close for a month and a day,
   'Mid thy grey books, and old inky papers ;
Then come here again when I show my bright face,
In the dress of the April with blossomy grace,
   And clear from the chill wintry vapours.

"Come when my vegetive wealth I may show
Of yellow primroses where tufted they grow
   To gather at will for thy pleasure ;
And when from dull books thou hast shaken thee free,
A merry May song I will witch out from thee,
   To sing to my sweet-purling measure.

"Come when my banks are all gay with the sheen
Of the light-waving twig tipt with virginal green,
   Where the breeze with the blossom may dally ;
Come with the friend of thy counsel the best,
Or with the dear maid that reclines on thy breast,
   By the bonny green burn o' Bonaly.

"Come with the memory, pleasant and sweet,
Of the mellow-souled judge, for his leafy retreat,
   Who trimmed the old tower of Bonaly ;
Whose heart was as kind as the old grass that grows,
Whose voice was as sweet as the water that flows
   Round the green ivy-tower of Bonaly.

"Come with bright thoughts like my fountain that wells
Round the grey-castled hall where the wise thinker dwells
   By the quiet green slope of the valley ;
And bathe thee in seas of the flowery perfume
That floats from the breath of the furze and the broom,
   By the bonnie green burn o' Bonaly."

Oban, 26th August 1880.

James Ballantine also was inspired by the charms of Bonaly Burn :—

BONNIE BONALY.

" Bonnie Bonaly's wee fairy-led stream
Murmurs and sobs like a child in a dream ;
Falling where silver light gleams on its breast,
Gliding through nooks where the dark shadows rest,
Flooding with music its own tiny valley,
Dances in gladness the stream o' Bonaly.

" Proudly Bonaly's grey browed castle towers,
  Bounded by mountains, and bedded in flowers,
  Here hangs the bluebell, and there waves the broom ;
  Nurtured by art, rarest garden sweets bloom.
  Heather and thyme scent the breezes that dally,
  Playing among the green knolls o' Bonaly.

" Pentland's high hills raise their heather-crowned crest,
  Peerless Edina expands her white breast,
  Beauty and grandeur are blent in the scene,
  Bonnie Bonaly lies smiling between,
  Nature and art, like fair twins, wander gaily ;
  Friendship and love dwell in bonnie Bonaly."

A PAWKY PENTLAND SHEPHERD.

To Graham, the author of the poem " The Sabbath," this was a favourite resort. Lord Rutherford has the following story told of him by Dean Ramsay, how he was rebuked by a shepherd, near Bonaly. He had entered into conversation with him, and was complaining bitterly of the weather, which prevented him enjoying his visit to the country, and said hastily and unguardedly, " What a d—d mist ! " and then expressed his wonder how or for what purpose there should have been such a thing created as east wind. The shepherd, a tall, grim figure, turned sharply round upon him, " What ails ye at the mist, sir ? it weets the sod, it slockens the yowes, and forbye," adding with much solemnity, " it's God's wull." Lord Cockburn himself was called to account, though for a more venial transgression. He was sitting on the hillside with the shepherd, and observing the sheep reposing in the coldest situation, he said to him, " John, if I were a sheep, I would lie on the other side of the hill." The shepherd replied, " Ay, my lord, but if ye had been a sheep, ye wad hae had mair sense."

LORD COCKBURN'S FRUITFUL SUGGESTION.

According to Principal Shairp, the idea of the Edinburgh Academy was suggested to Lord Cockburn as he trod the top of one of the Pentland Hills. " On the top of one of the Pentlands, the idea of a new classical school (the Edinburgh Academy) first flashed on the brain of Henry, Lord Cockburn. It was a fitting birthplace for a large and beneficent idea. Not in the retirement of the lawyer's study, not under his wig in the Parliament House, but under his rustic hat, with the free Pentland winds blowing about his manly and expressive face, that idea was born."

But we pass from Bonaly upwards towards Glencorse along the old bridle road, still used by equestrians. Isabella L. Bird (Mrs Bishop), the great lady traveller, once climbed one of these hills on horseback. The myriads of pedestrians who have gone that way, who can recount?—amongst them Professor Playfair and Lord Webb Seymour. Lord Cockburn used to envy them their Pentland walks together. Numerous, no doubt, in the middle ages, the path is now marked by streams of goers and comers during the season; nor is it solitary on this route in winter, or uninspiring at that time, as may be seen from the verses by Mr Will H. Ogilvie given on the back of the title page.

It is from the ascent to Bonaly reservoir that the "lion, splendidly sleeping, and the tall crags silent and grey," are seen to the east. At the summit of the watershed is a stile, which crossed discloses a descending path to Glencorse valley, whence we have a distant view of the Esk ravine, with the hills behind. On the left, up the Capelaw hollow, are the suggestive ruins of a cottage with trees, and on the right, further down, up the Loganlee valley, the Kips come into view, with Scaldlaw bounding the view.

HUGH MILLER ON GLENCORSE.

No one who has been alone in the heart of the hills here can forget the haunting charm of Castlelaw, Carnethy, or the Logan burn twinkling down the vale from Loganlee. Glencorse reservoir is an artificial lake receiving the Logan and Kirk burns, the Glencorse burn issuing at the other end of it. It was formed in 1822 as an equivalent for the loss of water sustained by the water mills on the Esk, and also for an addition to the water supply of Edinburgh. Of Glencorse reservoir Hugh Miller writes: "People at a distance, when they hear Glencorse reservoir called a Compensation Pond, might imagine it little superior to a tolerable horse one, with a submerged churchyard at its bottom, *infused* for the special benefit of our Edinburgh water-drinkers. But not such the character of the Compensation Pond. Let the reader imagine of it as marked by all the better characteristics of a genuine Highland loch in a genuine Highland glen, surrounded by bold steep banks, embosomed by hills varying from a thousand to nineteen hundred feet in height, with water much more than enough . . . Were an ordinary sized sloop to founder in some of the deeper parts of the Compensation Pond, the whole of the mainmast would disappear, and two-thirds of the topmast to boot."

STORY OF THE HUNT OF PENTLAND.

Sir Walter Scott, in a note to the "Lay of the Last Minstrel," thus relates the story of the founding of St Katherine's. "King Robert the Bruce following the chase upon Pentland hills, had often started a 'white faunch deer,' which had always escaped from his hounds; and he asked the nobles, who were assembled around him, whether any of them had dogs which they thought might be more successful. No courtier would affirm that his hounds were fleeter than those of the King, until Sir William St Clair of Roslin unceremoniously said, he would wager his head that his two favourite dogs, Help and Hold, would kill the deer before she would cross the March-burn. The King instantly caught at his unwary offer, and betted the forest of Pentland-moor against the life of Sir William St Clair. All the hounds were tied up, except a few ratches, or slow-hounds, to put up the deer; while Sir William St Clair, posting himself in the best situation for slipping his dogs, prayed devoutly to Christ, the blessed Virgin, and St Katherine. The deer was shortly after roused, and the hounds slipped; Sir William following on a gallant steed, to cheer his dogs. The hind, however, reached the middle of the brook, at which the hunter threw himself from his horse in despair. At this critical moment, Hold stopped her in the brook; and Help, coming up, turned her back, and killed her on Sir William's side. The King descended from the hill, embraced Sir William, and bestowed on him the lands of Kirkton,

Loganhouse, Earncraig, etc., in free forestrie. Sir William, in acknowledgment of St Katherine's intercession, built the chapel of St Katherine in the Hopes, the churchyard of which is still to be seen. The hill, from which Robert Bruce beheld this memorable chase, is still called the King's Hill ; and the place where Sir William hunted, is called the Knight's Field."

EDINBURGH WATER SUPPLY.

Edinburgh water supply originally came from draw-wells in the city, which in time became contaminated with sewage and too limited in quantity. The wells were thereafter supplemented by water from the South Loch, where are now the Meadows, according to a resolution made in 1598. By 1681, as mentioned in Route 1, Edinburgh had secured a supply from the Pentlands, taking it from Comiston. Forty years later other springs were added, and land purchased for the collection of the Swanston springs.

ST KATHERINE'S CHAPEL.

When the New Town began to be built, new springs were acquired at Bonaly and an installation formed in 1822, at Crawley and Glencorse. Telford and Rennie, the celebrated engineers, were responsible for the plans. The Bonaly ponds were afterwards abandoned ; their site may be noticed on the left hand of the ascent to Bonaly reservoir. The formation of Glencorse reservoir necessitated the submergence of St Katherine's Chapel, the foundations of which have been several times exposed in recent dry years, having been observed in 1835, 1842, and again in 1901. The ruins are 40 feet long by 20 feet wide, and about 18 inches high, with a hewn corner at the south-west angle. It stands due east and west, and in plan resembles Duddingston Church, but is five feet less in width. There is a tombstone at the south-east corner, 6 feet long by 3 feet 4 inches wide, with a plain shield in the middle, below that a date of 1623, and part of an inscription at the bottom of the lettering, which evidently read, " Blessed are the dead who die in the Lord " When the Chapel was submerged, the graveyard was fully a quarter of an acre in extent, and the boundary wall visible about twelve inches above the ground; the Logan burn running twenty yards south of the south boundary wall (remains of this wall may still be seen in a dry season about 20 yards south of the Chapel), and the March burn 20 yards east. In a letter in the *Scotsman* in 1898, another tombstone is referred to as a boulder-protected tombstone, erected to the memory of James Glendinning, bearing the date 1666.

The Chapel is referred to as existing in 1230, Henry de Brade making a gift in that year of the teinds from the lands of Bavelaw Castle to the monks of Holyrood for the support of the chapel of St Katherine of the Pentlands. It was annexed to the bishopric of Edinburgh, and added to Penicuik in 1635. It was named St Katherine of the Hopes ("hope" being a hollow among hills), probably in distinction to St Catherine's upon the Hill, at the Balm Well, near Liberton. The *Courant* stated in 1842 that it was not less than two hundred years since the church had been used.

In 1848, the Black Springs and those of Bavelaw and Liston Shiels were available, and Threipmuir and Harelaw in 1847-8, as compensation to the mill owners on the Bavelaw Burn and Water of Leith. Clubbiedean (1850), Torduff (1851), Loganlee (1851), and Bonaly (1853), were added, and in 1859, the Colzium Springs, at the source of the Water of Leith, were gathered into the Harperrig reservoir, partly as compensation and partly as city supply; then, in 1868, came the absorption of the Crosswood springs and the formation of the Crosswood reservoir.

In 1869 the Edinburgh and District Water Trust took the place of the old water authorities, and secured the springs which formed the Gladhouse reservoir, at the foot of the Moorfoot Hills. In the distant Talla valley, Peeblesshire, a reservoir, two miles long, has been formed, which can furnish Edinburgh with ten million gallons of water a day. This additional supply was made available to the city in 1905.

Edinburgh has thus water made available for the loftiest houses in the city without any labour of carrying; in contrast to the old system, where, in many parts of the " Old Town," people stood in groups patiently waiting their turn at the wells with pairs of wooden "stoups," which were carried in the hand, and kept asunder by iron hoops. Many of these wells have been retained as interesting mementoes of the old history of Edinburgh.

Return may be made by Route 1 reversed. From Glencorse Reservoir it is 8¼ miles by road to Edinburgh; Colinton to Balerno, by Loganlee, is 13 miles; Penicuik is 7½ miles from Colinton; Glencorse station is about two miles south from Reservoir.

Bonaly Tower.

CHAPTER VI.

Route 4.

FROM COLINTON TO JUNIPER GREEN, CURRIE, AND GLENCORSE.

Colinton to Currie or Balerno by Kenleith—Juniper Green—Baberton—Wood-hall—Dr John Brown's Gallop to Juniper Green—Currie to Glencorse—Currie (or Killeith)—The Old Inn—Currie to Lennox Tower and Malleny—Lennox Tower—Malleny—Famous Residents in Currie Parish—The Northern Skirts of the Pentlands.

COLINTON TO CURRIE OR BALERNO BY EAST AND WEST KENLEITH.

FOLLOW the Woodhall road past West Colinton House. The first road to the left, a Water Trust one, leads by Torduff and Clubbie-dean to East Kenleith, thence to Balerno. The next road on the left also leads by a path round the north side of Torphin Hill, for Balerno. Or if we reverse the route, take train to Balerno, and walk back to town by Kenleith, we reach the same point at East Kenleith farm, and may follow the footpath to the north of Torphin Hill. We go through Balerno, past the paper mill, take the first turn to the left, cross Bavelaw Burn, and approach the farm of Harelaw. We have a fine panorama of hills to the right, and to the left West Lothian to the Forth, unfolded before us ; nearer, the villages of Currie, Juniper Green, and Colinton ; the houses in the two last, with red-tiled roofs, stand out clearly. At East Kenleith farm, the path straight forward goes to the north-east of Torphin and joins the Woodhall road at Colinton. By turning to the right at Kenleith, at the top of Poet's Glen,

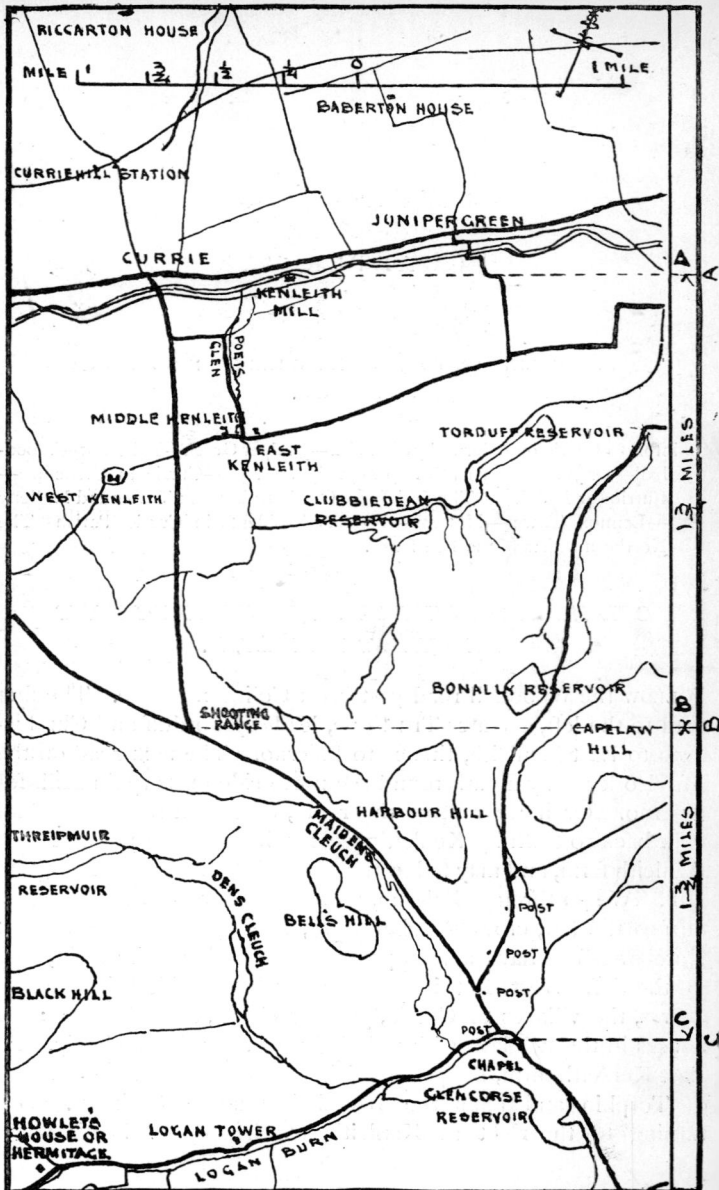

ROUTE NO. 4.

RICCARTON HOUSE

MILE 1 3/4 1/2 1/4 0 1 MILE

BABERTON HOUSE

CURRIEHILL STATION

JUNIPER GREEN

CURRIE

A A

KENLEITH HILL

POETS GLEN

MIDDLE KENLEITH

EAST KENLEITH

TORDUFF RESERVOIR

WEST KENLEITH

CLUBBIEDEAN RESERVOIR

1 3/4 MILES

BONALLY RESERVOIR

B B

SHOOTING RANGE

CAPELAW HILL

MAIDENS CLEUCH

HARBOUR HILL

THREIPMUIR

DENS CLEUCH

BELL'S HILL

POST

RESERVOIR

POST

POST

BLACK HILL

POST

1 3/4 MILES

C C

CHAPEL

GLENCORSE RESERVOIR

HOWLET'S HOUSE OR HERMITAGE

LOGAN TOWER

LOGAN BURN

and going round the north side of Clubbiedean and Torduff reservoirs, a fine bit of romantic scenery will be enjoyed. There is a miniature waterfall on the streamlet between the two reservoirs. On leaving Torduff, the view of Bonaly, Colinton, Craiglockhart, the Braids, and Arthur Seat beyond, is very fine. It was the view of Edinburgh from Torphin Hill which H. W. Williams said most resembled that of Athens. The Water Trust road (not a right-of-way) is followed from Clubbiedean, until the Woodhall road is reached, west of Colinton.

Waterfall above Torduff.

JUNIPER GREEN.

Those who wish to keep the main road for Route 4 may begin at Colinton, pass westward through Juniper Green, reaching Currie, ascend the Kirkgate, and from there by Malleny shooting range to Glencorse. Juniper Green is a modern village, first mentioned in the records in 1707. Robert Paul, the Edinburgh banker, noted in 1841: "Hugh Miller out with us at Juniper Green. Mr Sinclair came out in the boat." This was by passenger boat on the Union Canal to Murrayburn boathouse.

BABERTON—WOODHALL.

On the right, about half-a-mile away, is Baberton House, built by John Murray, the King's Master of Works, in 1623, in the style of Heriot's Hospital. The ex-King of France, Charles X., came to Baberton, for shooting quarters, while residing at Holyrood. His son, the Duc d'Angoulême, and the Duchesse de Berri with her daughter and son, and the Duc de Bordeaux, the King's grandson, were also with him. The date 1622 appears over one of the windows of Baberton House. The lands can be traced back to the fourteenth century, proprietors' names having been Cissor, Crawford, Forrester, Wardlaw, Elphinstone, and Sir James Murray, Master of Works to King James. In the circled pediment of one of the windows are the initials I. M. and K. W. About the time of the Revolution, there was a Presbyterian meeting house at Baberton. On the left is Woodhall, which gave a title to Hugh Cunningham, an advocate who became a Lord of Session in 1637, and took his seat as Lord Woodhall. Woodhall descended to Foulis of Ravelston. The Foulises were connected with George Bannatyne, of the "Bannatyne Collection" of Scots poems.

Between this and Currie are the Kenleith paper mills, and two snuff mills, which are said to be two out of the three left in Scotland. Before reaching Currie is the "Poet's Glen" on the left, so named from James Thomson, the Weaver Poet, who makes Water-o'-Leith Brigs speak, as well as his shed in the Glen. A well there has a verse from his poems inscribed upon it. Copper was discovered in 1608 near Currie, probably in the Poet's Glen, but the results of mining for it did not justify the outlay.

DR JOHN BROWN'S GALLOP TO JUNIPER GREEN.

Dr John Brown has related a gallop with his father to Juniper Green. "I was then a young doctor—it must have been about 1840—and had a patient, Mrs James Robertson, eldest daughter of Mr Pirie, the predecessor of Dr Dick in what was then Shuttle Street congregation, Glasgow. She was one of my father's earliest and dearest friends,—a mother in the Burgher Israel, she and her cordial husband 'given to hospitality,' especially to 'the Prophets.' She was hopelessly ill at Juniper Green, near Edinburgh. Mr George Stone, then living at Muirhouse, one of my father's congregation in Broughton Place, a man of equal originality and worth, and devoted to his minister, knowing my love of riding, offered me his blood chestnut to ride out and make my visit. My father said, 'John, if you are going, I would like to ride out with you;' he wished to see his dying friend. 'You ride!' said Mr Stone, who was a very Yorkshireman in the matter of horses. 'Let him try,' said I. The upshot was, that Mr Stone sent the chestnut for me, and a sedate pony—called, if I forget not, Goliath—for his minister, with all sorts of injunctions to me to keep him off the thoroughbred, and on Goliath.

"My father had not been on a horse for nearly twenty years. He mounted and rode off. He soon got teased with the short, pattering steps of Goliath, and looked wistfully up at me, and longingly to the tall chestnut, stepping once for Goliath's twice, like the Don striding beside Sancho. I saw what he was after, and when past the toll he said in a mild sort of way, 'John, did you promise *absolutely* I was not to ride your horse?' 'No, father, certainly not. Mr Stone, I daresay, wished me to do so, but I didn't.' 'Well then, I think we'll change; this beast shakes me.' So we changed. I remember how noble he looked; how at home: his white hair and his dark eyes, his erect, easy, accustomed seat. He soon let his eager horse slip gently away. It was first *evasit*, he was off, Goliath and I jogging on behind; then *erupit*, and in a twinkling—*evanuit*. I saw them last flashing through the arch under the Canal, his white hair flying. I was uneasy, though from his riding I knew he was as yet in command, so I put Goliath to his best, and having passed through Slateford, I asked a stonebreaker if he saw a gentleman on a chestnut horse. 'Has he white hair?' 'Yes.' 'And een like a gled's?' 'Yes.' 'Weel then, he's fleein' up the road like the wund; he'll be at Little Vantage' (about nine miles off) 'in nae time if he haud on.' I never once sighted him, but on coming into Juniper Green there was his steaming chestnut at the gate, neighing cheerily to Goliath.

I went in, he was at the bedside of his friend, and in the midst of prayer; his words as I entered were, 'When thou passest through the waters I will be with thee, and through the rivers, they shall not overflow thee;' and he was not the less instant in prayer that his blood was up with his ride. He never again saw Mrs Robertson, or as she was called when they were young, Sibbie (Sibella) Pirie. On coming out he said nothing, but took the chestnut, mounted her, and we came home quietly. His heart was opened; he spoke of old times and old friends; he stopped at the exquisite view at Hailes into the valley, and up the Pentlands beyond, the smoke of Kate's Mill rising in the still and shadowy air, and broke out into Cowper's words: Yes,

> 'He sets the bright procession on its way,
> And marshals all the order of the year;
> And ere one flowery season fades and dies,
> Designs the blooming wonders of the next.'

Then as we came slowly in, the moon shone behind Craiglockhart hill among the old Scotch firs; he pulled up again, and gave me Collins's Ode to Evening."

CURRIE TO GLENCORSE.

The route from Currie to Glencorse (4 miles) rises abruptly from 500 feet at the station to 757 at Kenleith Smithy, and after that the remainder of the four miles to Glencorse is pleasant walking, with Malleny shooting ranges on the left, and Harelaw and Threipmuir reservoirs on the right. It was up the Kirk Loan from Currie, and through Maiden's Cleugh, between Harbour Hill on the left and Bell's Hill on the right, that Dalziel of Binns rode towards Rullion Green (Route 1). This was of old the Drove Road to House of Muir market, Glencorse. Dr Jamieson, writing in 1845, calls Maiden's Cleuch, Cleughmaidstone, as being the pass to the Chapel of St Katherine, Glencorse, and having a font of water, in which the pilgrims washed before entering the Chapel of the Holy Maid of St Katherine. The route may be continued either to Edinburgh by Hillend, 8¼ miles, Balerno by Loganlee, Glencorse or Penicuik Stations.

CURRIE (OR KILLEITH).

Currie Church is a foundation of mediæval times, dedicated to St Kentigern or St Mungo, in 1296. In 1627, Currie was a special rectory and parsonage of the Archdeacon of Lothian, from whom it was taken and bestowed by King James VI. and I. on the city of Edinburgh. There is a monument in the churchyard to one of the pastors, Matthew Lichton, son of the first Protestant

Harelaw Reservoir.

minister of Currie, uncle to Archbishop Leighton ; a Templar's tombstone, with incised cross and sword, and two more broken stones within the church ; an ingenious sun-dial, the work of Robert Palmer, schoolmaster, is also worthy of attention. Palmer planned the old school-house, and painted the hemispheres on its gables for school use. Along with Sir William Gibson Craig, Palmer was originator of the Caledonian Curling Club, and started Currie Curling Club, which has a pond surrounded by trees on the moor. The Currie communion cups bear the marks of David

Heriot, who followed George Heriot as Deacon of the Craft, in the last year of the sixteenth century. A round hollow piece of silver, having remains of gilding on it, part of the stalk of a crucifix, or altar candlestick, was unearthed here after 1784, but has disappeared. Sir James Livingston of Kinnaird, captain of the guard, was stationed at Killeith, or Currie, when Dalziel of Binns went on his way to Rullion Green in 1666.

THE OLD INN.

The old-fashioned, two-storied, thatched house, standing at the north end of Currie bridge, is believed to have been the village ale-house, and a window at the east end was a handy place through which to dispense liquor. It is mentioned in James Grant's "Harry Ogilvie; or, the Black Dragoons." Anglers frequented the inn in the old days when kept by Marion Cunningham, about whom this rhyme has been preserved :—

> " At Currie brig end,
> Auld Marion was kend,
>   For forty years at least,
> By the great and the sma',
> The raggit an' bra',
>   The dominie, elder, and priest."

The deep water below Currie bridge gave rise to the saying, " As deep as Currie Brig," indicating shrewdness and selfish cunning.

The old mercat cross of Currie still stands on a slight eminence within Riccarton Woods. It is a square chamfered pillar, 3 feet 4 inches high.

CURRIE TO LENNOX TOWER AND MALLENY.

There is a fascination in By-Path Meadow. Immediately on leaving Currie station for the hills, the first road to the right has a ticket, " Private Road. No Thoroughfare." This is an estate road, and it may be as well to ask permission. Sir T. D. Gibson-Carmichael, while tenant of Malleny House, more than once repaired the bridge over Malleny Burn, and had no objections to well behaved pedestrians using the road. It leads straight to Balerno. Lymphoy House, with ivy-clad Lennox Tower and Malleny House, are passed on the right. The Bavelaw Burn is crossed, and Balerno is entered by a back road.

LENNOX TOWER.

A stringent Act was passed against poaching in 1594. Mr R. B. Langwill, in his notes on Currie Parish, mentions that six persons of this parish had to appear before the Privy Council for poaching on the Pentlands. They belonged to Whelpside, Riccarton, Warriston, and Currie, and were all convicted, when they were obliged to promise that none of their children, tenants, nor servants should, for all time coming, hunt with their dogs within the space of six miles of His Majesty's Castle of Edinburgh. Neither were they to keep hounds or dogs upon any condition whatever. Lennox Tower, Baberton, and Bavelaw are traditional

Lennox Tower.

hunting seats of James VI. The ivy-clad wall of Lennox Tower is 7½ feet thick. In its round-headed entrance doorway may still be seen the aperture for a sliding bar behind the door. It had a vaulted ground floor, a waggon-vaulted great hall above. Tradition has it that there was a subterranean communication with the Water of Leith and Curriehill Castle on the opposite bank, as also with Colinton Tower. Queen Mary and James VI. are said to have resided here. The Marquis of Montrose spent a night at Lymphoy on his way to the fatal field of Philiphaugh. There is a tradition that King James sold the tower to George Heriot, "Jingling Geordie," who in turn sold it to his daughter.

F

MALLENY.

The estate of Malleny, which was purchased by the Earl of Rosebery in 1882, belonged to the family of Scott, a branch of the Scotts of Buccleuch. Laurence Scott, Clerk to the Privy Council, held various estates near Currie, Harperrig, Buteland, Bavelaw, and Clerkington. The gardens are laid out in the Dutch style, and contain a number of fine yew trees and plane trees. The ivy-covered house dates from the end of the seventeenth century.

The Scotts held Malleny from the time of the first half of the seventeenth century, and perhaps they built the mansion, although it has an old carved stone over the kitchen chimney-piece with arms on it, the date 1589, and initials I.K., probably associated with the Knightsons of Malleny. When Lord Rosebery bought the estate, the family retained the mausoleum, which is not far from the mansion.

FAMOUS RESIDENTS IN CURRIE PARISH.

Famous residents in Currie Parish have been Sir John Skene (1543-1617) of Curriehill, who was one of those chosen to carry through the negotiations concerning the marriage of Princess Anne of Denmark with James VI. He was also one of the Commissioners to treat for a Union between England and Scotland, and published important legal books. Sir Thomas Craig (1538-

1608) of Riccarton, founder of the Craig family, was author of "Jus Feudale." His "De Unione" is still in manuscript. Margaret, his eldest daughter, married Alexander Gibson of Durie, and from this branch the present representatives are descended. Another daughter married James Johnston of Warriston, merchant of Edinburgh, one of his children being Archibald Johnston, a Presbyterian leader, executed in Edinburgh in 1663. His head was placed on the Netherbow, but was afterwards taken down and buried with his body in Greyfriars' Churchyard. Currie Memorial Hall is erected in memory of James Robert Gibson, second son of the present Baronet of Riccarton.

Other famous natives were James Anderson, LL.D. (1739-1808), writer on agriculture; General Thomas Scott (1745-1842) of Malleny; John Marshall (1794-1868), Lord Curriehill. Later residents are Dr George Keith, author of a "Plea for a Simple Life," and the late Dr William Smith, a President of the Philosophical Institution.

Larch Grove, and the Lodge, above Balerno, once belonged to Sir Alexander Morrison, specialist in mental diseases, and President of the Royal College of Surgeons. On one of the windows of Cockburn House is carved the date 1672. Ravelrig was once the property of Baron Graham.

THE NORTHERN SKIRTS OF THE PENTLANDS.

"These northern skirts of the Pentlands," says Mr John Geddie, "are something of a backwater in the national annals. The stream of great national events, swinging strongly round the eastern end of the range towards the capital, has taken a more northern line to the west. But great men and noteworthy deeds have not been wholly wanting. One need not go back to 'Old unhappy far-off times and battles long ago,' when forgotten warriors built their camps and cairns on the Wardlaw and Ravelrig Hills, or on the crest of the Kaimes. We know that kings feasted at Bavelaw, and winded the bugle-horn, and hunted hart and roe on Threipmuir; that moss-trooping Elliots and Armstrongs and Scotts have pricked thither on foray to lift the kye and gear of the Lothians' lairds and tenants, and escape back to Tweedside by the Boarstane Pass, or the Cauldstaneslap. . . . The Templars, and after them the Knights Hospitallers from Torphichen Preceptory, must have been not unfamiliar figures in the lands that belonged to them on the Water of Leith, now partly covered by Harperrig Loch."

Colinton Dell.

CHAPTER VII.

Route 5.

BALERNO BY LOGANLEE TO MORNINGSIDE.

A Winter Walk : Balerno to Glencorse—Kirk Road to Penicuik—Poetry and Provender—Howlet's House—Logan Tower—When Legs grow Weary.

[The first portion of this route may be traced in Route Map 6 ; then in 4 and 1 reversed.]

A WINTER WALK—BALERNO TO GLENCORSE.

WE describe a winter walk over this very popular route, which follows the same road as Route 6 till near Bavelaw Castle. The 10.30 a.m. train from Princes Street Station disgorged a goodly number of passengers at each station before Balerno was reached. There was a wonderful number brave enough on a certain New Year's Day morning to pass through Balerno, by Redford, Bavelaw, and by the Pentland pass that brings the pedestrian to the Logan Burn, Loganlee, and Glencorse. No Pentland walk is finer than this, but when there is a residue of snow on the path, and the hills are bewitching and fairy-like in a white mantle, only the bravest will venture. The day was fine, the air exhilarating, and the snow did little to hinder a winter tramp. How merry this mixed party of young folks are, and how tingling with life and energy in every limb, as they negotiate the winding path above Bavelaw. We might be a hundred miles from the city : there is Scald Law in front, where, tradition says, was the scene of the the gathering of old Norse minstrels, singing the songs of the Vikings and Berserks. James V. hunted around Bavelaw, and Queen Mary came over from Lennox Castle on the Water of Leith to hawk here. Covenanters, flying wounded from Rullion Green, fell, and tradition says their remains have been found in the moss here.

KIRK ROAD TO PENICUIK.

The ascent to the Kirk Road for Penicuik is made from Logan Burn, above Loganlee Cottage, and is marked by posts. The watershed is crossed between Carnethy and Scald Law, at 1456 feet, and after descending the Grain Burn, the Biggar road is reached, east of Silverburn.

Waterfall near Loganlee.

POETRY AND PROVENDER.

Below the waterfall at the head of Logan Burn is still frozen; its waters creep away with a muffled sound. Four adventurous spirits climb the steep bank and examine the conglomerate strata above the waterfall, in the burn, which is rather a rare outcrop on the Pentlands. What an exquisite view down towards Loganlee as we descend from the upper reach of the burn on this high plateau! Looking back, two black figures are seen struggling through the snow along the side of the Hare Hill; there, on the slope of Scald Law, and near the top, four more dark figures have almost conquered that eminence. A welcome halt at the waterman's cottage at Loganlee affords time for a rest and some refreshment. An array of teapots stand on the wall, for a party of ten is expected hungry from the hills. The empty churn has disgorged that flaky white butter on the plate, and the half-dozen rosy children who live here, four miles from the nearest school, and six miles from Penicuik, are enjoying themselves snowballing outside. The waterman's wife walked six miles on the day previous, when it was snowing, to sell her eggs and make purchases. While resting, one of the party reads from Mr Will. H. Ogilvie's recently-published little booklet of poetry, "Rainbows and Witches." "In Pentland Wine," cut from *The Scotsman*, is also read, and is so far in harmony with the scene, except that to-day all is quiet, and it is not true that

> " The west wind, wanton, is chiding
>   Glencorse with the scourge of his whips,
> And the wild duck over it riding
>   Are tossing like storm-tossed ships."

For the wild ducks pass above our heads, and a couple of grouse cross the upper end of Glencorse with gurgling discontent at being disturbed. All appreciate these verses of Ogilvie's, which come home in the silence of the hills here with new delight, making allowance for the winter season :—

THE KINGSHIP OF THE HILLS.

> " Born in the purple, the red grouse cry ;
> Born in the purple, the whaups reply ;
> Born in the purple, the clouds are kings
> Sailing away on their snow-white wings.
> The eagle high on the ruby peak
> Has the scorn o' the vale in his curling beak :
> And every hour that goes dancing down
> Has a purple robe and a silver crown.
> The lightnings flash like a jewel band ;
> The thunder rolls like a king's command ;
> With a palace roof of the windy stars,
> Where God looks over His golden bars,
> Here, in the pride of all high-born things,
> The red-deer go with the gait of kings ;
> And only a step from their cottage-doors
> The rough hill-shepherds are emperors."

HOWLET'S HOUSE.

On an eminence overlooking a burn flowing into Loganlee reservoir, is a ruin popularly called the " Howlet's House," but most likely the priests' manse belonging to St Katherine's Chapel of the Hollow, with its own chapel attached. Part of one of the vaulted roofs remains, with some of the original plaster upon it. This vault was complete in 1877. It is to be hoped that the remains will be preserved. The ruin is charmingly situated on the rocky bank, and looks down on an undergrowth of bushes with rowan trees, which margin the streamlet on its northern side.

Loganlee Reservoir.

LOGAN TOWER.

One mile from Glencorse reservoir are the ruins of Logan Tower, an ancient keep which belonged to the St Clairs of Roslin from very early times. The Barony of Pentland and Pentland Moor was given to Sir Henry St Clair by Malcolm Canmore for his services against the English invaders. In 1681 Logan House and Kirkton lands, with tower and fortalice, passed by purchase from the St Clairs to Alexander Gibson. In 1782, they came into possession of William Ferguson of Raith, and in 1831, of William Robertson, who sold them to Charles Cowan, M.P., about 1852.

They are still in the possession of the Cowans of Penicuik. All that remains of this ancient keep is the vaulted ground floor, 20 ft. by 17 ft., having its entrance at the side, with a hypothetical date, 1230, upon its lintel, cut in the nineteenth century.

WHEN LEGS GROW WEARY.

At Loganlee we are about 10 miles by road from Edinburgh, and we are below the shadow of Carnethy, and face Castlelaw, which blocks the valley to the eastward, and are now on the road leading round the south of the Pentlands, by Easter Howgate, towards Hillend and Lothianburn. It is a short-cut, though not a right-of-way, to skirt Castlelaw, climb along past Castlelaw Farm, and by the policies of Woodhouselee pass out on to the old Biggar road, at Easter Howgate. The main road winds pleasantly and deviously past Glencorse reservoir and Flotterstone Bridge. By the time we are back to town fourteen miles (including that detour on the hill behind the waterfall) have been negotiated since leaving Balerno. But the way is shortened by story-telling, and one who has just returned from Spain relates an endless narrative of his adventures and misadventures, with a visit to the Alhambra thrown in. The glories of the Alhambra pale before a well-earned evening meal, and there was the calm satisfaction in the breast of each that "something attempted, something done, had earned a night's repose."

Harelaw.

CHAPTER VIII.

Route 6.

The Currie Route—Threipmuir—The Monk's Road—G. M. Kemp.

ROUTE 6, between Balerno and Nine-Mile-Burn, is 7 miles, and is similar to 5 on to Bavelaw.

TO JOIN THE CURRIE ROUTE FROM BALERNO.

Near the top of Balerno village, if we take the road to the left, past Malleny Mills, with Balleny Farm to the right, at Harelaw Farm, by a gate on the moor, the path from Currie station may be joined, leading to Glencorse reservoir. At Harelaw, near the present farmhouse, there stood at one time a cairn, which, having been removed within recent times, disclosed a cist containing human bones; to the south were five tall stones set up vertically; many stone coffins were found at the bottom of the field, and these and the cairn are supposed to indicate the site of a battlefield. A stone was erected to mark the spot where the coffins were discovered, by General Scott, who died at the advanced age of 96. He distinguished himself in the American War by carrying important dispatches in his rifle, dressing himself as a pedlar, and so passed through the enemy to the British forces at the other side. For this service Lord Melbourne rewarded him with a handsome pension.

THREIPMUIR.

For Nine-Mile-Burn, we follow the road to Bavelaw, reaching the old ruined farmhouse of Redford, which lies on the left. We cross the bridge at Threipmuir reservoir. This name, according to the old story, already quoted, arose when Sir William St Clair of Roslin staked his head against his hounds, when hunting with King Robert the Bruce, and *threeped* the dogs in pursuit of a white deer. The notes of encouragement were successful ; St Clair's head remained on his shoulders ; he received a grant of the forest of Pentland from the king, and in gratitude founded the Chapel of St Katherine of the Hopes at Glencorse. Threipmuir, and Harelaw further east, which is on a lower level, are compensation ponds, and the former has been raised to meet the needs of the Water of Leith Purification Scheme. It is the headquarters of an Edinburgh angling club.

A pleasant avenue, which has been well called the Gate of the Pentlands, leads past Bavelaw Castle, the teinds on the lands of which were given by Henry de Brade, during the reign of William the Lion, in favour of the Monks of Holyrood for the support of St Katherine's of the Pentlands. In the course of changes of ownership, the castle came into the possession of Robert Mowbray of Barnbougle in the sixteenth century, and, about 1600, to Laurence Scott, one of a younger branch of the Malleny Scotts, already referred to ; and later, in 1783, into the hands of the Johnstones, merchants in Gothenburg. It is now the property of Mr John S. Tait.

Avenue, Bavelaw.

THE MONK'S ROAD.

The path forward leads to Loganlee (Route 5) : we follow that to the right, which at length takes us to the watershed at the base of the West Kip. Here again are two diverging paths : that to the left leading by Eastside Farm in the direction of Penicuik. We pursue that to the right, to Nine-Mile-Burn, past the Monk's

Rig, on which is the base of an ancient cross, which marked
the pilgrimage way between the monastery (which stood at New-

ROUTE 5 ND 6.

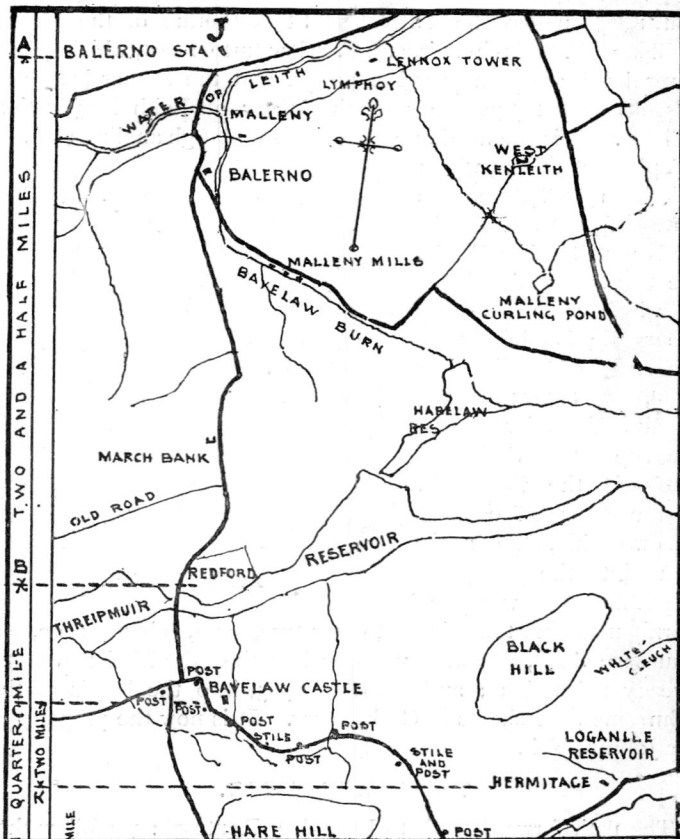

hall) and Queensferry. In 1835 some old copper coins were
found under the socket of the cross. To the south, on the other
side of the Monk's Burn, is the farm of "Spittal," an outpost
of the monastery, which wayfarers used to visit for supper and

a night's accommodation, as monastic usage led them to expect. It is only right to admit that there is neither documentary nor

ROUTE 5 AND 6—continued.

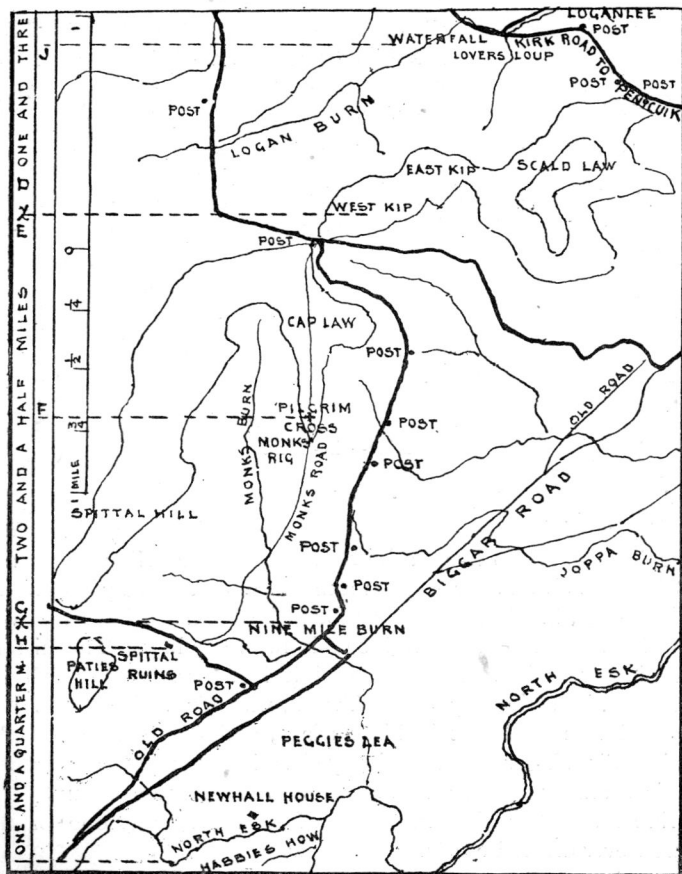

architectural evidence to prove there was a monastery at New-hall. But the names, Monk's Rig, Monk's Road, Monk's Burn, and Monk's Haugh, and also the farm called Spittal, are strong evidence in favour of the supposition. The ruins of an old hospice may be seen near Spittal farm, north of Nine-Mile-Burn. The inn here is on the old coach road which passed to Carlops.

Nine-Mile-Burn.

G. M. KEMP.

George Meikle Kemp was an infant when his father, a Moorfoot shepherd, came to live on the Newhall Estate at Nine-Mile-Burn. Being sent on one occasion on a message to Roslin by Mr Brown of Newhall, in his tenth year (1806), he seems to have received the impression that determined his future calling. The history of his career is well known, and it is interesting to recall his meeting, in the valley of the Tweed, with Sir Walter Scott, who invited him to a seat in his carriage, and drove him to Gala-shiels, Sir Walter enthusiastically describing the Border ecclesiastical antiquities to one who was to design the monument in Princes Street, which Professor Masson said was one of the finest ever erected to a man of genius.

At the cross-roads, Walstone, near Nine-Mile-Burn, the distances by main road are: to Edinburgh by Penicuik and Newington to G.P.O., 13 miles; Edinburgh by Flotterstone and Morningside, 12¼; Penicuik, 3½; Carlops, 2; West Linton, 5 miles.

CHAPTER IX.

Route 7.

BALERNO TO CARLOPS.

Traces of the Templars—The Bore Stone—Newhall—Scenery of the "Gentle Shepherd" around Carlops—The Original MS. of the "Gentle Shepherd."

TRACES OF THE TEMPLARS.

FROM Balerno to Carlops by the Bore Stone is $9\frac{1}{2}$ miles. In this route between Balerno and Carlops, there is first a walk of two and a half miles along the Balerno or old Lanark road westward till the turn southward, near "Boll of Bear," can be made in the direction of Listonshiels, and thence on to Carlops, passing the North Esk Reservoir. A nearer way is to pass through Balerno, and follow the road to Bavelaw, turning off westward along the old road just beyond Marchbank. This road joins the path at Listonshiels. On the first way to Listonshiels, by the Lanark road, we pass Temple House, and may observe Temple Hill to the west, reminding us that the Templars at one time owned much of the land in this quarter. In fact, they had possessions in almost every county in Scotland. Sir James Sandilands, who built the choir of Midcalder Church, was the last Grand Prior of the Hospitallers, and joined the Reformers in 1560. The Order was then suppressed, and Sir James, on paying a sum down, and engaging to pay an annual rent to the Crown, entered into possession of the remaining estates in that quarter as a temporal barony, and was created Lord Torphichen. Listonshiels was at one time attached to Kirkliston Church, and as its name implies, was probably a place where "shiels" had been erected for the shelter of the flocks and herds belonging to the patrimony of the Church.

THE BORE STONE.

At the post, the summit of the pass, we are 1300 feet above sea level. The Bore Stone is the extreme north point in the boundary

ROUTE NO. 7.

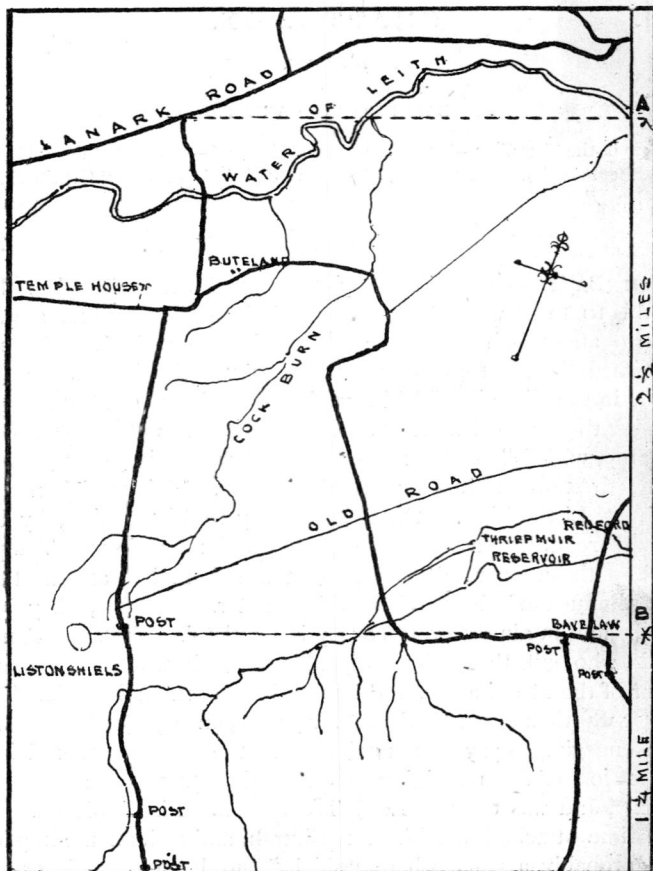

line of Peeblesshire, and the north-west limit of Penicuik estate. To the west rise the Cairn Hills; past the watershed, and before the

North Esk Reservoir is reached, in a glen opening into the East Cairn Hills, on the right, at the top of a valley, an Edinburgh lawyer built a house about 1750, which no longer exists. At the

ROUTE NO. 7—continued.

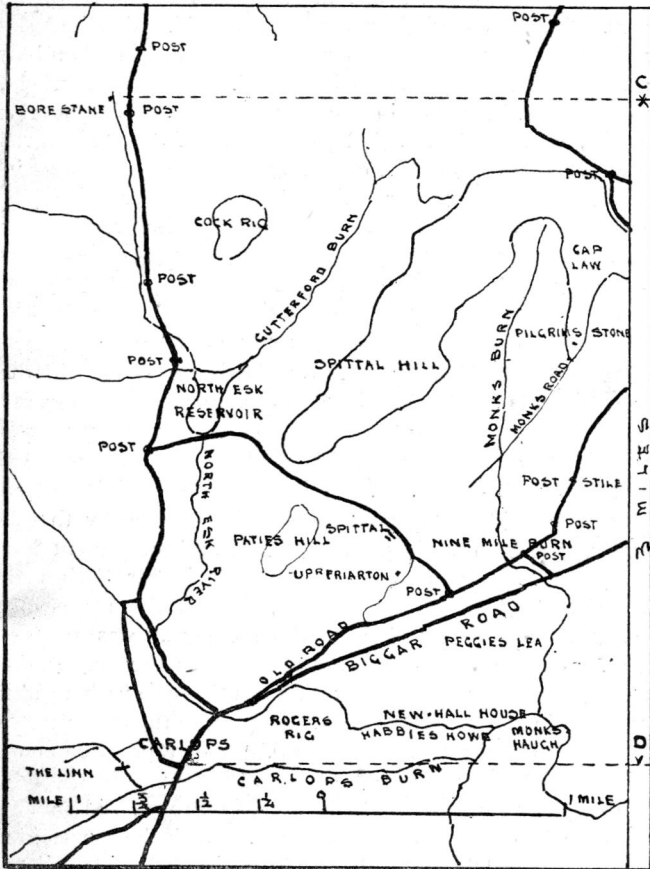

snug cottage at North Esk Reservoir (which belongs to Penicuik papermakers), it is sometimes possible to receive welcome refresh-

G

ment. The path on the east of the stream is of a truly Highland character, until the old mill and the waterfall are reached, close to the Biggar road. Below the reservoir, on the left, a path leads east over the Saddle to Nine-Mile-Burn.

The village of Carlops was in the olden time occupied by weavers. Below its bridge was a woollen mill. On the Esk at Marfield was a flax mill, and further up a fulling mill and dye-house. At Gladsheugh was a bleachfield, and near Marfield, a gunpowder mill, blown up in the year 1830, some of the workers, unhappily, being killed. Carlops is now a favourite resort of trippers, who come by cycle, coach, or motor. For cyclists it is an ideal run by Penicuik, or Hillend, to the village. The North Esk here marks the boundary between Peeblesshire and Mid-lothian.

NEWHALL.

The lands of Newhall were granted by Robert III, early in 1400, to Laurence Creichtoune, and his descendants held them till the beginning of the seventeenth century. Dr Alexander Pennicuik acquired Newhall in 1646; his son Alexander was author of a " Description of Tweeddale." In 1703 it became the property of Sir David Forbes. In the beginning of the eighteenth century most of the old place was pulled down by the then possessor, Mr John Forbes, an advocate, and the present house built by him. It was the popular resort, in Mr Forbes' day, of many of the leading literary men, among whom was Allan Ramsay, whose poem, " The Gentle Shepherd," was published in 1725. Of the various places suggested as the scene of the poem, Newhall has the strongest claim as the spot " where a' the sweets o' spring and summer grow," and where runs the "trotting burnie wimpling through the ground." Other proprietors were the Hays and Browns (1783).

One of the proprietors, Hugh Horatio Brown, did much to beautify the grounds, and identify the place with the scenes in the " Gentle Shepherd." In the library at Newhall there is a painted ceiling showing Allan Ramsay and his brother worthies. Dr Horatio Robert Forbes Brown, eldest son of Hugh Horatio Brown, who has a reputation for books on Italian subjects, has had the unique experience of having had several manuscripts accidentally burned at different times, including his popular "Life in the Lagoons." He has written for the "Cambridge Modern History," and is author of "Studies in the History of Venice."

At Habbie's How.

SCENERY OF "THE GENTLE SHEPHERD" AROUND CARLOPS.

An illustrated booklet published more than half a-century ago, in possession of the publisher of this book, furnishes views of this neighbourhood identifying it at every turn with Allan Ramsay's "Gentle Shepherd." There is a portrait of Allan Ramsay in the front, with nose elongated as much as is the case in Captain Elliot's sketch of the poet John Leyden. It is from a picture in Newhall House. The views include the Fore Spital of New-hall, with the Pentlands behind; Newhall House, with a distant

view of Simon's farm; Habbie's House; Lin Burn; Washing
Green behind Newhall House, with maidens near a wash-tub:

> " A flowery howme between twa verdant braes,
>   Where lasses used to wash and spread their claes,
>   A trotting burnie, wimpling through the ground,
>   Its channel pebbles shining smooth and round."

Then there are Glaud's farm and entrance to Habbie's How,
with the motto:

> " Gae farer up the burn to Habbie's How,
>   Where a' that's sweet in spring and summer grow."

On the North Esk at Carlops.

Next are Habbie's How from the Washing Green; Harbour Craig, near the Craigy Beild, where field preachings still take place; Upper Lin of Monk's Burn behind Glaud's Farm; Mause's Cottage and Roger's Habitation above Habbie's How; Simon's Cottage, over the Esk, from Marfield Loch, with Carlops Hill in the distance. We mention this as an interesting curiosity, without pronouncing on the locality, a point left un-
settled by the only one who could settle it, the author of the
poem. The probabilities, however, seem to rest with the North
Esk, at Newhall, Carlops. Edinburgh has had its monument to
the poet for many years. Sir James Clerk erected in 1759 a
memorial with inscription in the grounds of Penicuik House.

THE ORIGINAL MS. OF "THE GENTLE SHEPHERD."

An enthusiastic Edinburgh collector has the original MS. of "The Gentle Shepherd," which is a folio volume of 105 manuscript pages, bound in yellow russia leather, just as presented by the poet to the Countess of Eglintoun. There is a note in the handwriting of Sir Alexander Boswell, son of Dr Johnson's biographer, to whom it belonged, dated 1804, which is as follows: —"This MS. was presented to my father (with flattering expressions of regard) by Susanna, Countess of Eglintoun, the last time he visited her. I have preserved the original binding to show the form in which Allan offered it at the shrine of Susanna. I have put 1725 as the date, though the dedication appears to have been '35, and altered by the author to '25." Ramsay's plain old-fashioned handwriting throughout is very legible. Here and there, at the close or beginning of the Acts, the author has amused himself by adding comic pen-and-ink sketches. When published it met with extraordinary success. There is this note at the close: "Finished the 29th of April 1725, just as eleven o'clock strikes, by A. Ramsay. All Glory be to God. Amen!"

Broomlee Station (West Linton), is 3½ miles from Carlops; Penicuik Station is 6 miles.

CHAPTER X.

Route 8.

MIDCALDER TO WEST LINTON BY THE CAULDSTANE SLAP.

Little Vantage—Water of Leith—Colzium and Cairns—West Linton—Routes
West of Cauldstane Slap—Covenanter's Grave.

ROUTE NO. 8 may be said to begin at Midcalder Station, from
which the starting-point on the Lanark Road may be reached. It is
13 miles to Broomlee Station, West Linton. Midcalder itself has a
very interesting old Parish Church, which is said to have been
founded by Duncan, Earl of Fife, the then Lord of the Manor,
in 1215, but there is no part of the church so old as that. From
the Earls of Fife, from whom it had its old name of Earl's Calder,
the Manor passed to the Douglasses, and from them about the
middle of the fourteenth century, to the knightly house of Sandilands. A younger son of the sixth Knight of Calder, and parson
of the parish, laid the foundation of the choir, and raised the
walls of the vestry before 1542. The transepts at the west end,
which complete the church, are modern.

Ascending from the Calder valley, and after a three-mile walk,
we reach the Lanark road, turn to the right for three-quarters of a
mile, passing the ruined inn called "Little Vantage," and then go
southward towards the Cauldstane Slap. About a mile down we
reach the Water of Leith, here a small stream crossed by stepping-
stones. As there is neither bridge nor ferry, the pedestrian in
times of "spate" will have to go a little further up to the reservoir,
and cross by the road there. So that this route, although pursued
by enthusiasts in all seasons, is for the ordinary pedestrian only
for summer use. It may here be mentioned that another method
of approach is from Balerno, instead of Midcalder, along the old
Lanark road, a very fine walk of five miles, sometimes through

avenues of trees, and again in the open, with spacious views southwards of the Pentland range, across either a well-wooded valley or, as it may be, bare moorland. We shall pass on this road some of the old change-houses of coaching days, " Boll o' Bear," " House of Muir," and as already mentioned, the half-way house of " Little Vantage."

But having reached by either route the stepping-stones of the Water of Leith, we notice on the right, Harperrig reservoir, into which the infant Water of Leith with its tributaries discharges. At this point are the ruins of East Cairns Castle, which in its prime belonged to Sir George Crichton, High Admiral of Scotland, and Earl of Caithness, who charged himself with warding this pass of the Cauldstane Slap through the Pentlands, which in later times became the drove road, most commonly frequented by dealers conveying sheep and cattle between the Scotch and English markets. In the good old times it was used by freebooters from the south, Scotts, Armstrongs, and the rest, who so late as 1600 took eighty cattle, besides horses, southward with them after wounding and killing those who tried to prevent them. In 1582 the occupants of East Cairns suffered, at the hands of Armstrong and Liddell, the raiding by night of ewes and wedders which lay at Hairhope.

Colzium, which lies further south, together with Cairns and other properties, came into the hands of Mr Michael Linning, W.S., in the early part of the 19th century. He was a subscriber to and Treasurer of the scheme for building the National Monument on the Calton Hill, towards the erection of which he offered in 1830 as much stone as would complete it from a freestone quarry, which he discovered in the West Cairn Hill. He had also a scheme for using the peat on the moor as a fuel, and anticipated some ideas, only realised in recent times, for utilising the Leith's head waters for the Edinburgh water supply, and for supplementing the water power of the various mills. In 1598, Colzium, which had a tower, was raided of cattle by Scott of Branxholm's men, some of the cattle being however returned to the owner. Stevenson, in " Weir of Hermiston," brings in " the four black brothers of Cauldstane-slap."

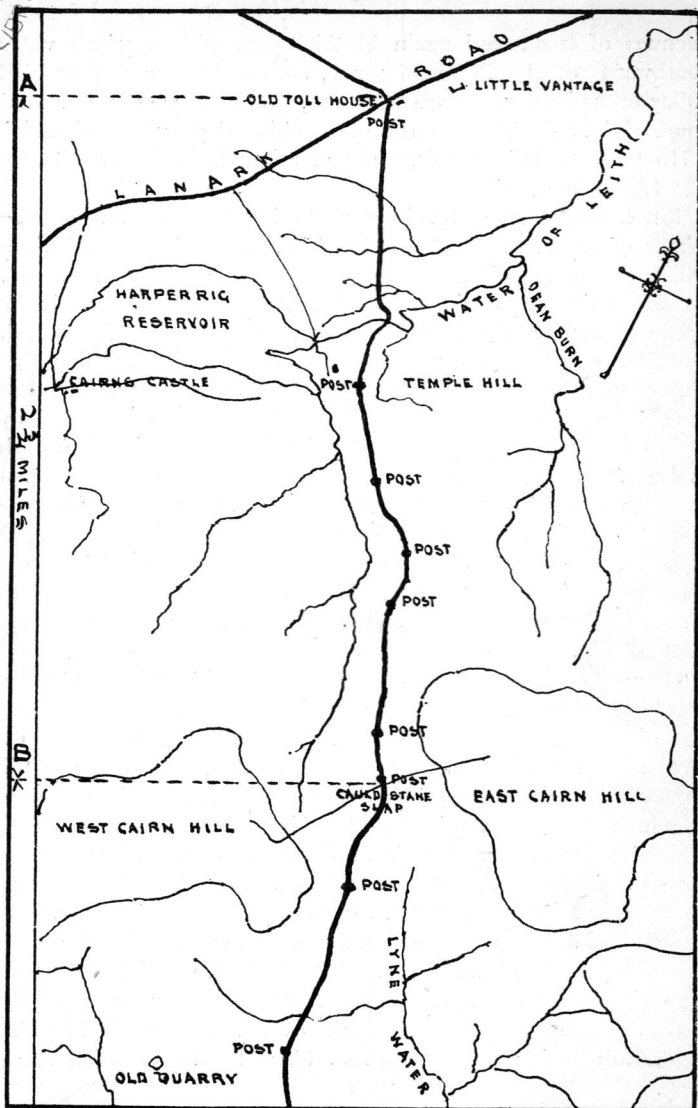

ROUTE NO. 8.

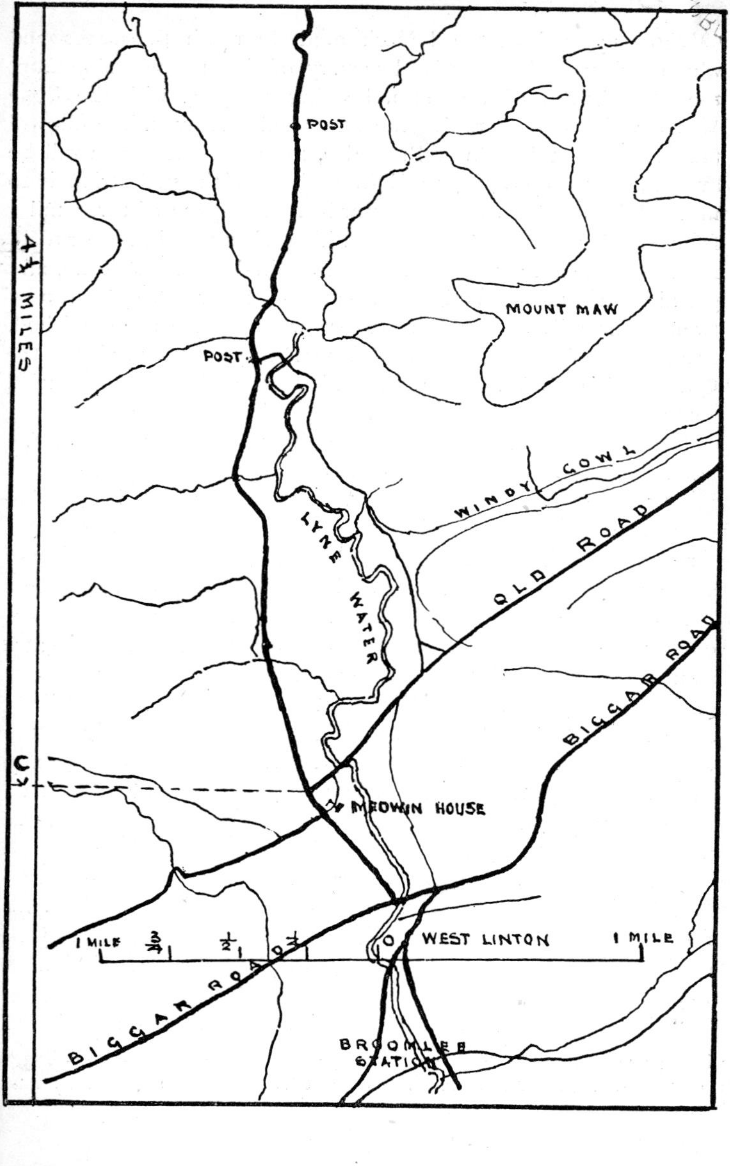
4¼ MILES
POST
POST
MOUNT MAW
LYNE WATER
WINDY GOWL
OLD ROAD
BIGGAR ROAD
C
MEDWIN HOUSE
1 MILE ¾ ½ ¼ 0 WEST LINTON 1 MILE
BIGGAR ROAD
BROOMLEE STATION

Three miles from the Lanark road we reach the water-shed which separates the moorland scenery of the northern side from the more sylvan of the south, keeping company with the Lyne Water, which has its rise at the watershed. A five-mile walk will take us to West Linton or Broomlee, from whence a train will be available for easy return to Edinburgh, or if the pedestrian is so minded, he can turn south-eastwards after a space of three miles from the Cauldstane Slap, and find himself on the old Biggar road, from whence he may go back by Nine-Mile-Burn to Balerno, and get his return there, making a circuit from Balerno to Balerno of twenty-four miles, which one of the writers once accomplished. Another keen pedestrian started from Dunsyre station, visited the Covenanter's Grave, and walked along the hills to Edinburgh, some 26 miles.

Linton, we believe, means the village by the water or the pool. Dr W. Chambers has done justice to West Linton in his " History of Peeblesshire." West Linton, which has a golf-course, and has been growing in recent years, is a popular resort for summer visitors. The crystal Lyne, noted for the number of stone coffins and tumuli found on its banks, flows past the village. The houses in the village, as far as order and arrangement are concerned, might have dropped from the clouds. In the centre stands the Lady Gifford's Well, surmounted by a puffy-faced stone effigy of that personage, originally set up in 1666 by Laird Gifford, a mason and stone-carver. This image is all that remains of the original well, which was renewed in 1861. There is a legend to the effect that James Oswald of Spital or Spittals, an estate among the Pentland Hills, now included in the estate of Newhall, was accidentally shot by his servant while out after wild ducks at Slipperfield Loch. Oswald, who was of a very sociable and hospitable disposition, possessed a hall table of marble, on which his festivities were conducted. This table was used as his tombstone (which has now disappeared), with the following inscription, as here translated :—

" This marble table, sitting at which I have often cultivated good living (propitiated my tutelar genius), I have desired to be placed over me when dead. Stop, traveller, whoever thou art ;

here thou mayst recline, and, if the means are at hand, mayst enjoy this table as I formerly did. If thou doest so in the right and proper way, thou wilt neither desecrate this monument nor offend my manes.

"Nov. 28th, 1726. " Farewell."

John Hay Forbes, the second son of Sir William Forbes, the eminent Edinburgh banker, purchased the estate which lies around Medwin House on the Lyne. All the family have been great benefactors to the locality.

On the Baddingsgill Burn, near West Linton.

The interior of the parish church is more beautifully decorated than most country places of worship. A part of the walls and the front of the gallery are covered with chaste carved woodwork, with here and there a choice text of Scripture ; this was the work of Miss Fergusson, daughter of the late Sir William Fergusson, surgeon to the late Prince Consort, and author of a "System of Practical Surgery."

ROUTES WEST OF CAULDSTANE SLAP— COVENANTER'S GRAVE.

For the routes west of the Cauldstane Slap consult a good Pentland Map; we can only indicate them here. From Harburn Station to Dolphinton or Dunsyre the distance is about 13 miles. Distance by rail from Princes Street Station (Caledonian) to Harburn, is $15\frac{1}{4}$ miles. Follow main road from Harburn Station south to Lanark road, near Crosswood Reservoir, which is $18\frac{1}{2}$ miles by Balerno Road from Edinburgh. Follow path and right-of-way posts to right of Crosswood Burn farm house. At Garval Syke, 6 miles, is the source of Medwin Water; the Covenanter's Grave is on the left, at Blacklaw Hill. The story of this Covenanter is as follows:—The fugitive had called at a cottage on the Medwin Water, above the present mansion of Garvald, and, wounded and weary as he was, he could not be dissuaded from pressing on for Lesmahagow, whither he was returning. His strength had soon failed him, for about a mile from where he had called he was found dead on the moor, and was buried in the moss as he lay. This occurred on probably the 29th or 30th of November 1666. Rullion Green was fought late in the day of the 28th. About a hundred and sixty or more years after, his remains, wonderfully preserved from having lain in the peat, were disinterred and re-buried on the Black Law, where a stone marks the spot.

The inscription on the stone reads thus :—

Sacred
To the Memory of
A Covenanter
who fought and was wounded at Rullion Green
November 28 1666
And who died at Oaken Bush the day after the battle
And was buried here
by
Adam Sanderson of Blackhill.

The Covenanter's Grave may be reached most quickly from Dunsyre, by Easton farm, and following the path which takes to Crosswood and Harburn. From West Linton, by striking off beyond Medwin House, along the drove road, past North Slipperfield and Medwinhead. Two miles from Medwin House an old road goes south-west to Dunsyre, thence to Newbigging, and on to Carnwath, crossing the Medwin Water and the West Water. West Linton to Auchengray or Carnwath, about 15 miles.

These moors were the centre of Covenanting gatherings. The Rev. Donald Cargill preached his last sermon on the common of Dunsyre; William Veitch of Westhills, and Learmonth, the Laird of Newholm, leaders at Rullion Green, were from this quarter.

A field meeting was held on the first day of June 1684, at the Cairn Hill, and again seven days later at "Caldstaine-slope or some other place thereabout," to the number of three hundred men and women. The "pulpit rock" behind the West Cairn Hill at the Way-field crags was traditionally said to have been the rostrum from which the audience was addressed.

At West Water (9 miles), the path to the right by Easton farm leads to Dunsyre Station. For Dolphinton keep West Water on right, and Garvald House, to Dolphinton Station (27½ miles from Waverley Station).

CHAPTER XI.

THE OLD LANARK ROAD.

BY JOHN GEDDIE.

Proposed Highway through the Hills—West of Little Vantage—Traces of the Romans—The Thieves' Road—Notable Travellers—The Stage Coach—Other Memories of the Road.

THE Lang Whang is the bleakest portion of Carnwath Muir, and James Ballantine sings :—

> " O dreary ' Lang Whang,' wi' your auld brown muirs,
> Your deep black mosses, and heigh grey hills,
> Whaur the winter snaws and the summer showers
> Swell into rivers the drizzling rills,
> Dear, dear, are your cauld bleak braes to me,
> As ilk weel-kenned howff meets again my e'e."

It was in 1823, when the stage-coach was in its glory, that a proprietor of Cairns, the Rev. Dr Laird of Portmoak, disposed of the ground on which stood the sheep-cotes on the old Lanark Road, for the erection of an inn, to be called the Cairns Castle Inn. In these days of local veto agitation, the transaction might seem an odd one for a man who became a distinguished Disruption divine to have a hand in ; but Dr Laird, who was notable for his " truly rational assigning to doctrine and moral duty their appropriate places," had doubtless the approval of the more easy and genial conscience of the early nineteenth century for the act. They looked at such matters differently then ; and, besides, the conditions of " the road " have entirely changed since the coming in of the Steam Age. The little wayside change-houses and taverns, each of which was a snug centre of local incident and interest, have been swept off the face of the country roads ; and after them have gone the toll-houses that to some extent perpetuated their trade and fulfilled their functions. The school-house has come in their place; and this inn at Causewayend, after having provided entertainment for half-a-century for weary travellers, has descended, or ascended, to the position of an elementary academy of youth.

It is still an interesting relic of the old coaching days—one of several strewn, mostly in ruins, along the old Lanark Turnpike. There is reason to believe that for not less than fifteen or sixteen centuries the road and the stream have kept each other company. For a dozen miles or more they are close neighbours, and nothing that concerns the one has ever failed to be of interest to the other. On the road the current flows both ways; it has been the channel of the history, as well as of the traffic, that has passed up and down the Water of Leith. But in our days, what with the drain of the railways and other causes, it is a channel that begins almost to run dry before it gets so far to the west, and so near the hills, as Causewayend.

PROPOSED HIGHWAY THROUGH THE HILLS.

For the range of Pentland makes a third in this companionship. It provides an atmosphere and a background for the life of the Road and the story of the Water. It is from their neighbours the hills that these draw their most distinctive colour and flavour. The old Lanark Road bounds the Pentlands on their colder side, as the old Biggar Road does on the slopes turned towards the sun; and between these skirting highways lies a province of nature, sacred as yet from steam and even from wheels—a province that throughout its length of twenty miles or more is penetrated only by an occasional footpath or bridle-track. Once, indeed, a project was formed for running a highway across the range, making use, for the purpose, of that deep depression, the Cauldstane Slap, between the East and West Cairn Hills. It was to have made a direct way of communication between Tweedside and Lothian, following the line of the old "Thieves' Road" past Linton, which a hundred years ago, and down to a much later date, was still much used by drovers on their way to and from the trysts by the Forth. On the northern side, the scheme had got so far as the building of a viaduct on the Linnhouse Water, not far from Causewayend, which strides over a brook into a pathless moor, and "like a broken purpose hangs in air." Pedestrians only, and of these but a sprinkling, now cross the stepping-stones on the Water of Leith below the dam and sluices of the reservoir, and passing the farmsteading of Harperrig, follow by the guide-posts over moss and hill the track once so familiar to reiver and drover, smuggler and gipsy.

The old Lanark Road has not suffered the fate that, on the farther side of the hills, has overtaken its "marrow" on the way to Biggar; it has not dwindled, peaked, and pined, and got overgrown with grass and interrupted by cattle gates and stiles until at last nothing is left except a green terrace running athwart the hill slopes. It is still, so long as it holds close company with the Water of Leith, a well-kept highway—a road that is chequered with light and shade. Trees in clumps and lines are gathered about it: the bristling shield of the fir or the clean limbs of noble beeches stretch overhead, but never so closely but that we get peeps down into the dell of the stream and away to the wavy line of the Pentlands, or on the other side a glimpse or two of the broken outline of the Kaimes and Dalmahoy Craigs. With every turn or rise there is a fresh vista of tree-screened road, merging in the distance into purple-green if the leaves are out, or into purple-blue if there is snow on the ground. Nor is the element of human life and habitation wanting—old mansion-houses, like Ravelrig, with parks and doocots and rookeries; isolated farmhouses like West Haugh or Whelpside, nodding over the bed of the stream, yet keeping an eye on the highway; and groups of roadside cottages, with roses growing at the porch and children playing about the doorstep, as at Sunnyside.

WEST OF LITTLE VANTAGE.

But beyond the broken walls of what was once Little Vantage Inn, begins the bare and inhospitable stretch of road known as the "Lang Whang." If you come out upon it at any point between Auchinoon Hill and Carnwath, it is like that you may cast your eyes east and west on a long white ribbon of road drawn athwart moor and hillside, with no figure of man or four-footed beast in sight. Or, if the time be winter, and there has been a fall of snow, you may find, although the day be well advanced, that no dint of wheels, no footprint except that of *maukin* or moorcock, has yet sullied the white hap on this half-deserted high-road. After leaving Currie and Balerno Brigs behind on its westward way, it gets nothing to feed it except a few inconsiderable crossroads and cart-tracks to hill-farms, until passing the "kail yards" of Crosswoodhill it has climbed over the cold high ridge of the Maidenwell Brow, that takes it 1100 feet above sea-level, and has descended by Tarbrax far down into the Vale of Clyde. It is thrown upon its own slender resources, and the Caledonian Railway, running within sight at a lower level, has acted upon it like a leak in an ancient aqueduct, draining away its whole life and life-purpose.

A writer in *The Scotsman* has unburdened himself of a wallet of memories concerning the Lang Whang. He dwells upon its pre-eminent healthfulness :—" I once met, within a space of half-a-mile, four men who were all beyond the patriarchal age of eighty. Their wives also were living, all of them had seen the jubilee of their marriage, and one of them had celebrated his diamond wedding a few years previously. And near the same place was a healthy veteran of ninety, who was like unto Moses, for his eye was not dim nor his natural strength abated. He could read the newspapers without spectacles, and his tread was as firm as that of a man in his prime." The time to see the barer part of the Whang at its best is, he holds, the month of August, " when the endless range of heather stretches away on every side, with the sun shining on it and imparting to it a golden glory that makes it seem a place of enchantment. The stillness is intense and unbroken, except by the bleating of a sheep or the whirr of the moorfowl as they are started by the unwonted sound of the foot-step of the passer-by. You look before you and the road seems endless, varied by no turnings or windings among hidden places. For trees there are none. The highway, by reason of infrequency of travel and utter neglect, is becoming fast obliterated or deformed by huge ruts that are left uncared for. A solitary bicyclist is striving to make his way over the difficult ground, but has frequently to dismount and push his vehicle before him, wondering how the adventurous wheelman that made a journey round the world accomplished such a feat if much of the world was like the Lang Whang."

TRACES OF THE ROMANS.

Thus the stream and the road that for many miles, through many ages, traced between them the common border of civilisation and of the wild life of the moors, have lain open on one side —sometimes on both—to the incursions of the spirit of adventure. If history has been shy of it, romance has not seldom travelled by this quiet way under the hills to and from Lanark. The first-comers of which we have any word are supposed to be the Romans. Causewayend is believed to mark the termination of a paved way built in this direction by the great roadmakers and conquerors of antiquity. One hesitates to speak of Roman stations and camps, for towards these the modern antiquary is showing himself a very Edie Ochiltree in scepticism and prosaic explanation. But even if we shake the head over *Castellum Gregis*—" Watch Tower of the Flocks "—as the interpretation of Castle Greg, there is difficulty in getting over the evidence of the fragments of Roman pottery and the coins of Vespasian, Hadrian, and Marcus Aurelius that have been dug up at this place, which lies a couple of miles beyond Causewayend. And if we once grant that the legions threw up these entrenchments, it is possible to believe that the same masterful hands formed the original camps on Ravelrig and Kaimes, and even to find some speciousness in the conjecture of the elder tribe of antiquaries, who were confident they had found in Corston Law or in Currie the site of the Damnonian " Coria."

THE THIEVES' ROAD.

It is a far cry across troubled centuries from Roman times to those when, opposite the supposed sites of stations of the legionaries, rose strong fortalices to keep in awe the freebooters who might break in across Pentland by way of the White Craig, the Thieves' Way, the Borestane Pass, or the Currie Kirk Road. And all through those years it was never safe travelling the lonely moorland highway. Then, when the ploy of the mosstroopers ended, there came those racings and chasings of the conventicle holders ; and other people who had a quarrel with the law had also for a while their day on the Lanark Road. It was a true smuggler and gipsy route ; escape from it and to it was easy. The Rev. Dr Nisbet, minister of Currie, gravely discusses and laments, in the Old Statistical Account, the depopulation that had fallen on his parish a century ago, through the suppression of the communities of illicit traffickers who passed goods across country from Ayrshire to the East. The " howffs " of vagabond clans of Baillies and Faas also lay within handy reach of the road,—for instance the "auld ruinous waste house at Blyth," at which they organised raids into East Lothian, and made the base of a siege of Penicuik House. That " Gentleman Gypsy," Captain William Baillie, whose headquarters were at Biggar, must have been known only too well on the " Lang Whang" when last century was young ; he could act at will the ruffling gallant, or "the robber, the sorner, and the tinker " ; and "rode in scarlet," mounted like a nobleman, his sword by his side, and his leash of greyhounds following him. A drop of the blood of this truculent gipsy man descended to Jane Welsh Carlyle ; it may possibly help to explain the note of discord and unrest in the household of Cheyne Row.

NOTABLE TRAVELLERS.

Other notable personages, quick of eye and ready of hand, with history before or behind them, have come or gone by this way,— Bothwell and Montrose, Dalzell of Binns, plucking fiercely at his great vowed beard, and Donald Cargill, an undaunted captive, although his face were set in scorn to his horse's tail and his legs tied under its belly. With those of actual history mingle the figures of romance ; Sweet Willie of the ballad going to keep fatal tryst with May Margaret,

" As he rade o'er yon high high hill
And down yon dowie den,
The noise that was in Clyde Water
Would feared ten thousand men— "

is as real for us as William Lithgow at the end of his wanderings,
is over thirty-six thousand and odd miles," lamenting the barren-
ness and lack of planting which this region presented to the eye
when Charles the First was King, but rejoicing when he leaves
the moors, and approaches the neighbourhood of his native
Lanark, "all which," says he, a glow of local patriotism breaking
through the coxcombry of his style, " being the best mixed
country for corns, meads, pasturage, woods, parks, orchards,
castles, palaces, divers kinds of coal and earth fuel that our Albion
produceth, may justly be surnamed the Paradise of Scotland."

Margaret Lyndsay, too—Christopher North's Margaret—trod on
foot the " houseless moor " beyond Causewayend, looking anxiously
ahead for sight of Carnwath and " Tintock tap "; a July walk, for
" every moment there was something that delighted her ; the
green lizard, as it glided through the rustling tall grass by the wayside ; the lapwing, now less wily that its young are fledged, walking along the leafields with its graceful crest ; the large yellow-
circled ground bees booming by in their joyful industry ; the
dragon-fly, with her shivering wings shooting in eccentric flight,
almost like a bird of prey ; the bleating of the lambs on the sunny
knowes." Nor does one forget Carlowrie, of " the Black Dragoons," knocking at " the small change-house that stands at the
bridge-end of Currie," with the sign " Dundee threid, Edinburgh
breid, and new-laid eggs, by me, Lucky Legget, Ailbrowstar," and
bringing to the threshold the wrinkled old dame, clad in the curch
with long lappets and the short-skirted gown.

THE STAGE-COACH.

These are pictures from more peaceful times, when the stage-
coach was already on the road for those who could afford to use
it. The stage continued to roll, a dusty meteor, along the old
Lanark Road for years after it had been driven off the more

crowded highways. In the year that the Cairns Castle Inn was built, the coaches ran three times in the week by this route into Clydesdale, starting from inn-doors in the Grassmarket and Princes Street, and the first change of horses was at Tarbrax, four and twenty miles, after a long stiff pull over the Maiden Hill. But there would be frequent halts to take up and put down passengers, with time for refreshment and exchange of news, at Currie, at Little Vantage, and other places on the way. One seems still to hear a lingering echo on the road of the notes of the coach horn, the crack of the whip, the jingling of the harness, and to catch a faint vision of the smoking team, the driver stretching his stiff limbs and thawing his red nose in a stiff tumbler of grog while horses were fed or changed, and the passengers hurrying in to enjoy for a few seconds the light and warmth of the Cairns Inn before facing the cold bare ride across the " Whang."

There were other regular visitants on the line of the Lang Whang, on wheels and on legs. " Carts," says the writer already quoted, "conveying articles of various kinds passed to and fro ; shepherds, with the never failing plaid and crook and collie ; farmers, taking a survey of the state of their flocks and herds, were often to be met with ; and pastoral and agricultural life, even in those remote regions, was much in evidence. Twice a week, for the long period of forty years, there trudged along it a carrier who was known by the name of 'the cadger,' whose arrival at a 'farm toun' always was the cause of much noise among the canine inhabitants and interested bustle among those of higher degree ; for the cadger brought to them luxuries from the distant city, in exchange for which he got butter and cheese and all kinds of country produce, which in due time were exposed for sale in the market for such produce, which at that time was in the neighbourhood of the Tron Kirk. Seated serenely on the top of his high-piled cart, the cadger pursued his way with the leisured pace of former days, exposed to all the vicissitudes of the weather. In winter his case must have been a trying one, and only custom could have made the cold endurable. For in these regions protection there is none, and when 'the winter wind blaws cauld,' it blows with a will, penetrating to the very vitals."

Travellers of note and weight must often have looked down from the coach roof into the valley of the stream, where men famed in medicine, law, and literature lived or held holiday. On the Water of Leith and the Lanark Road colonies of lawyers have been planted from time immemorial alongside of its millers—powdered wig beside dusty coat. Let no one think that it is suggested that either class are the lineal representatives of the reivers and the gipsies of old; both can afford to snap their thumbs at the proverbs that assert that they have their gowpens in other men's girnels. But it is a fact that dynasties of judges and pleaders and writers, as well as of barley millers and paper-makers, have succeeded each other in the district. Behind Sunnyside, the Maconochies, once Campbells of Inverawe, took up quarters in the beautiful demesne of Meadowbank (at Kirk-newton), the first of them to sit on the bench being that Alan Maconochie who was one of the six who founded the "Speculative Society." Next neighbour was the "Courteous Cullen," also a Lord of Session and an active inspirer of the literary movement in Edin-burgh at the close of the 18th century, and the stooping form and keen eyes of Cullen's father, the great physician and chemist, must have been well known in the Road and by the Water, after he had left his Lawnmarket Close to Deacon Brodie and ill-fame and returned to the woods of Ormiston.

OTHER MEMORIES OF THE ROAD.

Nearer town there were yet more celebrated homes and playgrounds of men learned in the law and in affairs of State; Curriehill and the Skenes and Marshalls; Riccarton and the Gibson Craigs; Colinton and Woodhall and the Foulises; and, a more genial memory than any, Bonaly and Lord Cockburn. Wig, cocked hat and court sword, the lumbering old family chariot and the meteor-like fly have disappeared like the Romans and the raiders and have left only a faint memory; even the drover, the packman, and the gaberlunzie have become rare or extinct since the old days. The quaintly named wayside rests sprinkled thinly along the road beyond Balerno—the "House on the Muir," Little Vantage, the Half-way House—have been wiped out or turned to other uses. "Boll o' Bear" still keeps its name and its place on the edge of the road, where a strip of marshy moor separates it from the Dalmahoy Hills. One must not expect to find there any remembrance of the time when, as noted in Foulis's "Account Book," the road-side changehouse was the scene of a jolly "pennie wedding," to which, at the desire of the Laird of Dalmahoy, the Lord Torphichen, the Baronet of Ravelston, and doubtless other county magnates were invited, the while troopers were hunting Covenanters in the mosshaggs behind the Cairn Hills.

But one looks for some recollection on the spot of the last recorded of the lawless doings on the Lanark Road. In the "Resurrectionist" times, the churchyards accessible from this highway were favourite haunts of the ghouls who brought the dead from the grave to the dissecting room ; and Currie had to build its watch-house and Colinton provide its "janker." In the late evening of a winter day in 1821, a cart, containing a couple of corpses stolen from Lanark churchyard, covered with peats and straw, drew up at the successor to the "Boll o' Bear"—"Jenny's Toll" at the ninth milestone. The accepted account runs that the cart had been noted in its out journey by two stone-breakers, and its lightness having given rise to suspicion, its return was watched for. But local tradition asserts that the body-snatchers were heard talking about their gruesome cargo through the thin partition of Jenny's bar-room, where they had drawn up to refresh themselves. Help was summoned from Balerno, and Mr James Craig, overseer of the Balerno Paper Mills, and Mr Elliot, the exciseman—in those days an indispensable adjunct of paper-making—came to the rescue. Thomson, the Currie bard, tells in his doggerel, how

> " Near Currie town brave Elliot met them,
>   And ae fit farder wadna let them,
> Fast by the reins he seiz'd the horse,
>   Craig search'd the cart, and a' by force."

The sequel was a grand entertainment "to Lanark's praise and

Currie's glory," defrayed by the grateful burgh that had its corpses intercepted and restored to it, and attended by "as much conviviality as the circumstances of the melancholy cause of the meeting would admit of."

Avenue near Woodhouselee.

CHAPTER XII.

ROUND THE PENTLANDS IN ONE DAY.

The Birds and Birds of Passage—Associations of Biggar Road—W. E. Gladstone's Ancestry—Dr John Brown—The Lang Whang—Lord Rosebery's Motoring Experience—Down Grade to Edinburgh.

THE distance as we did it runs to fifty-five miles, the route taken being by Morningside, Lothianburn, the old Biggar road by Woodhouselee, Glencorse, West Linton, Dolphinton, Elsrickle, Carnwath, and then by the "Lang Whang" along the old Lanark road by the north side of the Pentlands, which brings us towards Edinburgh by Crosswood, Causewayend, and Balerno. At an earlier period, we made the journey, on the tricycle, more painfully, by Leadburn, Romanno, Biggar, Liberton, Carnwath, and back by the Lang Whang and Balerno, which made the road ten or twelve miles farther. This time we do the journey by cycle. By leaving the Biggar road at Melbourne, and mounting the gradual incline towards Elsrickle, and on to Carnwath, there is a saving of several miles as compared with going round by Biggar.

THE BIRDS AND BIRDS OF PASSAGE.

We can only indicate the wealth of interest awakened by the sights and scenes of this circular tour round the Pentlands and back to Morningside. R. L. Stevenson and Swanston have had sufficient attention in earlier chapters, but the four of us had less thought of Lothianburn Golf Course or Swanston than for the meteorological aspects of the day, to which a south-east wind might give birth. The three young men scorn waterproofs. One is a young ornithologist, and keeps us perpetually awake to the wonders of fresh nests in hedgerow, dyke, or hedgeroot. There is a partridge's nest near the ford above Glencorse Church, at the hedgeroot, which had four eggs when we saw it last. We do not go near it to-day.

But another at the hedgeroot before Flotterstone Bridge is reached is examined. It had two eggs a week ago, and lo! Mrs Partridge has laid seven eggs more, for there are nine now, nicely covered with dried grass and leaves from prying eyes. That is a good week's work. We restore the dried grass and leaves, and hope a mother's cares shall see fruition. A blackbird has built in the dyke beyond Flotterstone Bridge—one can see the four blue eggs in passing; and a little higher up a robin's nest has young ones. The birds are a perpetual delight. There is the note of the cuckoo and lark, and the sight in passing of the blackbird, thrush, bullfinch, crows, black-headed gulls, lapwings, blue tits, and jack-daws. There is a gullery near Slipperfield Loch, beyond West Linton, where the black-headed gulls perpetually fly and scream. They are noisy to-day. When we saw the place two years ago, a little earlier in the season, and leapt over the boggy ground from tussock to tussock of grass, we saw nest after nest with one, two, or three eggs in each. We were rewarded by very wet feet and an interesting experience. Enough of the birds, however, for we are birds of passage ourselves to-day!

ASSOCIATIONS OF BIGGAR ROAD.

If the historical or literary associations be uppermost, then one recalls, as we have already done, how Christopher North escaped from Edinburgh on the Dumfries coach, and was bowled along to his favourite pools on the Tweed, near the Crook Inn; and how Thomas Carlyle journeyed to and fro by Erickstane and the Devil's Beef Tub to or from Ecclefechan. How he hated the journey! Woodhouselee recalls the Tytlers and early visits from Walter Scott after he started housekeeping near Lasswade. We have time to think of the battle of Rullion Green on the hillside to our right while climbing upwards out of Glencorse Glen, where Sir Thomas Dalzell defeated nine hundred westland Covenanters on November 28, 1666 (Route 1). The father of George Meikle Kemp, architect of the Scott Monument, was a shepherd at Nine-Mile-Burn. There are associations with Allan Ramsay at New-hall, and his "Gentle Shepherd" has lent undying lustre to Habbie's How, which we passed on entering Carlops.

W. E. GLADSTONE'S ANCESTRY—DR JOHN BROWN.

And here too we may say that the western end of the range has its own memories, as, for instance, of the forebears of Mr Gladstone, who was descended from the Gledstanes of Arthurshiel in Lanarkshire. A certain William Gledstanes, who came to live in Biggar in 1679, was Mr Gladstone's great-great-grandfather. The names of several of them are recorded on tombstones in Biggar Churchyard, and Mr Gladstone as a boy, about 1829, interviewed a watchmaker there, of the same stock. Dr John Brown wrote "Rab and His Friends" as a lecture for his native Biggar, and felt that he read it but badly: when published the Doctor found sympathetic friends all over the world. And never had a father's memory a finer tribute than that which he wrote, "done to the quick," in his well-known "Letter to John Cairns, D.D."

THE LANG WHANG.

Our lunch by the North Medwin is a feast for the gods. We have had four hours' riding and walking, and our appetites are in fine trim. Instead of a Hillend, as at the east end of the Pentlands, here, at the west end, we pass Kame End, ere we race down into Carnwath. One word about the surface of the road along the Lang Whang, which we begin to negotiate as we leave Carnwath. The road has no surface: it is worn to the bone by spring rains and winter storms where not covered with reddish or gray roadmetal. It is a road to be avoided by the motorist or cyclist, unless once or twice in a lifetime as an experience. This is our third journey, and the loneliness, the sharp moorland air, the cry of the whaup, bleating of sheep, frolic of the young black-faced lambs, are as characteristic as ever. It is hard to believe that this road, with a tumbledown cottage here and there, and where the sight of a human being is almost an event, was the coach road from Edinburgh to Lanark.

LORD ROSEBERY'S MOTORING EXPERIENCE.

It is worth recalling that in the winter of 1906-7, Lord Rosebery was stranded on Carnwath Moor during a snowstorm through the breakdown of his motor car, while on the journey of forty miles to Dalmeny, from Glengonner House, Abington, where he had been lunching with the King. He passed Carnwath about 5 p.m., and when five miles further on, going up the "Lang Whang," his car ceased to work owing to the melted snow getting in about the works. He was only accompanied by his chauffeur, and after leaving the car on the moor, they faced the storm on foot back to Carnwath. The first house reached was the gate house at the entrance to Kersewell House. Lord Rosebery arrived at the lodge quite exhausted and alone, the chauffeur having been left some distance behind. His Lordship at once sent back a rescue party to bring in the chauffeur. The lodge-keeper took his Lordship up to the Kersewell House, where he was hospitably received, and remained for the night. He returned to Edinburgh on the following morning by train, none the worse for the adventure.

DOWN GRADE TO EDINBURGH.

We have been in three counties to-day—Midlothian, Peebles, and Lanark. At a lonely cottage, on the edge of the moor at Maiden Hill, the county boundary between Midlothian and Lanarkshire runs along the east gable of the house. We have a welcome rest and cup of tea here, as picking our way over the stony road and walking so much is very fatiguing. We see Tarbrax oil-works smoking below, and a Caledonian train ploughing its way westward beyond Cobbinshaw Loch. The most Tom Thumb-like station we have ever seen is that on the branch line from Carstairs, by Dunsyre, to Dolphinton, which we passed. Fancy Caledonian and North British Railways running to Dolphinton without shaking hands !—that is to say, running in connection.

From the thirteenth milestone, opposite Harperrig Reservoir, it is an easy descent to Edinburgh.

CHAPTER XIII.

A FAMOUS SOUTH PENTLAND STORY.

Ruskin's Association with Pentlands—The Writing of " Rab and His Friends "
—James and Ailie—Rab's Grave.

An experience of Dr John Brown's, author of " Rab and his Friends," at Juniper Green, is given on an earlier page. What follows relates mainly to the east and south side of the Pentlands. His brother, Professor Crum Brown, once said that the most characteristic thing Dr Brown ever wrote was the " Letter to John Cairns," descriptive of his father and his own early home at Biggar. Using one of his own expressions, it was "done to the quick." Both Ruskin and Jowett spoke highly of it.

The man who had room in his heart for all good men and dogs was also on friendly terms with John Leech, Thackeray, and John Ruskin, and his residence at No. 23 Rutland Street, Edinburgh, was a shrine of rare interest, whither strangers would come from far and near to visit the placid, bald-headed, bespectacled veteran, as he appeared then in later life. A Greek New Testament was one of his chief literary treasures. This book, his great-grand-father, the author of the Bible Commentary, got from a professor in the shop of a St Andrews bookseller, because, though he was then but a shepherd lad, the professor found he could actually read it. About 1846 Dr Brown was a dark-haired stoutish man, with fine soft eyes, spirited movement, and very benignant manner, the husband of a beautiful young wife.

His first clear recollections of his father, afterwards minister of Broughton Place U.P. Church, Edinburgh, dated from his fifth year. On May 28th, 1816, he had been sleeping with his sister Janet, in the kitchen bed with the servant, when they were all awakened by a cry of pain,—sharp, insufferable, as if some one had been stung. It seemed to these young minds, as they remembered it afterwards, to be like the great cry which arose at midnight in Egypt. The two young folks ran out in their night-clothes to the little room where father and mother slept. There stood the Rev. John Brown erect, "his hands clenched in his black hair, his eyes full of misery and amazement, his face white as that of the dead. He frightened us." The father, seeing he had frightened his children, taking his hand from his head, said, "Let us give thanks." When they turned to a sofa in the room, there lay their mother dead. She had slipped out of bed in a feverish fit, and expired there.

His early recollections were not all of this painful sort. While sleeping with the divine, he would sometimes awake in the early hours of the morning and see his father's keen beautiful face bending over some volume of divinity. The fire would be out, and the grey dawn peering through the window. Then he would come to bed, and take young John Brown, warm as he was, into his cold bosom.

In his writing and practice as a medical man, he was an apologist for the good old virtues of common-sense, practical clear-sightedness, and "vigorous rule of thumb," and essentially anti-speculative. He had an unusual apprehension of all that was good and admirable in character and life. His love for the lower animals was well known. "'Rab and his Friends' and 'Our Dogs' have been read," says Professor Masson, "by perhaps three millions of the English population of the earth; the very children of our Board Schools know the story of Rab and his friends. Who could have told the story like Dr John Brown? Little wonder that it had taken rank as his masterpiece, and that he was so commonly spoken of while he was alive as the Author of 'Rab and his Friends.' It was by that story, and by those other papers that might be associated with it as also masterly in their different varieties, as all equally 'done to the quick,' that his name would live. Yes, many long years hence, when you and I and all of us are gone, I can imagine that a little volume will be in circulation containing 'Rab and his Friends' and 'Our Dogs.'"

RUSKIN'S ASSOCIATION WITH THE PENTLANDS.

The publication in 1858 of the first series of " Horæ Subsecivæ " made its author famous, containing as it did the ever-popular " Rab and his Friends." We might call this a Pentland idyll, because Rab's home lay to the south of the Pentlands, and the author lived until his twelfth year at his native Biggar, where it was first delivered as a lecture in the Athenæum there in 1857. John Ruskin, after reading it, wrote to the author saying that it had given him " one more melancholy association, like a real one, with the Pentlands." Another reference is not so easily understood, when Ruskin said that he did not recollect anything that had given him " greater pleasure than the account of the Doctor's Sisyphian labours and ratiocinations on the Pentlands," in allusion to Dr Brown's article upon Dr Chalmers in the *North British Review* in 1848.

THE WRITING OF "RAB AND HIS FRIENDS."

The story of " Rab and his Friends " was founded on an experience Brown had as Professor Syme's assistant, in December 1830, in the old Minto House, which stood in what is now Chambers Street, Edinburgh. More than twenty-five years afterwards, Dr Brown had been invited by his uncle, the Rev. Dr Smith of Biggar, to lecture in his native town. He had never lectured before, and was puzzled as to what to give. The old incident of the carrier and his wife often came to his mind ; he tried to set it down, at first in vain. At last, after returning from a happy dinner at Hanley, near Gogar, he sat down on a midsummer night at twelve, arose at four a.m., and " slunk off to bed satisfied and cold. I don't think I made almost any changes in it. I read it to the Biggar folk in the schoolhouse, very frightened, and felt I was reading it ill." When it was published the Biggar folk liked it better, and it did a great deal for the doctor's growing reputation as an author. The real name of the Howgate carrier was not James Noble, but James Jackson ; and his wife was not Ailie Graeme, but Ailie (Alison) Tod ; and there are other purely imaginative touches.

There must have been more than one manuscript. One was burned by Dr Brown; another had these unprinted lines at the close: "I have in my head a human and a dog moral, if thought advisable, but I prefer every one being his or her own moralist.— J. B." In all likelihood this was the manuscript bought in a London saleroom by Quaritch for forty pounds.

JAMES AND AILIE—RAB'S GRAVE.

There is a pathetic passage in the story in which Brown describes the carrier bearing his dead wife Ailie from Old Minto House to his home, about a hundred yards to the northward of the level crossing at Pomathorn, now on the Peebles railway, although there was no railway in those days:—"I heard the solitary cart sound through the streets, and die away and come again; and I returned, thinking of that company going up Liberton Brae, then a' ng Roslin

Muir, the morning light touching the Pentlands, and making them like on-looking ghosts; then down the hill through Auchendinny woods, past 'haunted Woodhouselee', and as daybreak came sweeping up the bleak Lammermoors, and fell on his own door, the company would stop, and James would take the key, and lift Ailie up again, laying her on her own bed, and, having put Jess up, would return with Rab and shut the door."

Beyond the Pentlands, too, is Rab's last resting place :—" He was buried in the brae-face, near the burn; the children of the village, his companions, who used to make very free with him, and sit on his ample stomach, as he lay half asleep at the door in the sun, watching the solemnity."

Ruins of Old Woodhouselee.

CHAPTER XIV.

THE GEOLOGY OF THE PENTLANDS.

Carboniferous Strata—Denudation—Pentland Silurian Rocks—Fossils—Conglomerates and Sandstones—Volcanic Rocks—Volcanic Necks—Upper Old Red Sandstone — Carboniferous System — Old Red Sandstone — Geological Features on Balerno Railway—Silurian Rocks at Bavelaw—On Carnethy—By the Kips to Nine-Mile-Burn.

THE following notes on the geology of the Pentland Hills are based chiefly upon information obtained from the maps, sections, and various memoirs by Sir Archibald Geikie, together with some observations made by the Geological Survey. These were prepared by Dr B. N. Peach and the late Mr J. G. Goodchild, for excursions of the Geological Section of the British Association when in Edinburgh in the autumn of 1892. The material has been revised and brought up to date, and the results of later researches have been added, with an original contribution by Dr Peach on the "Development of the Pentlands" and regarding the effects of the "melt-waters" of the ice sheet.

CARBONIFEROUS STRATA—DENUDATION.

The Pentland Hills represent, in a highly modified form, part of the surface over which some thousands of feet of the Carboniferous rocks originally extended. Some time after the close of the Carboniferous period, the whole district of the Lothians underwent considerable disturbance, which in the neighbourhood of Edinburgh mainly took the form of a series of anticlines and synclines, whose axes lie from north-east to south-west. The present range of the Pentland Hills corresponds in a general way with one of these anticlines, whose eastern limb is dislocated by a large strike fault, the effect of which is to tilt the Carboniferous rocks on the east side of the Pentland axis at very high angles next the fault, while they gradually flatten out as they recede from that line of disturbance; and, along the Dalkeith Coalfield, they take the form of a large synclinal. On the opposite side of the Pentlands the Carboniferous rocks in general dip at a much lower angle, and lie naturally on the older rocks without any dislocation worthy of note.

Some time after the disturbances just referred to had taken place, denudation of the Carboniferous strata commenced, and was prolonged through a period of sufficient length to effect the removal of all those rocks from the highest exposed parts of the Pentland anticlinal; the old precarboniferous floor—folded up as the core of the anticlinal, and flanked on its south-eastern side by the large fault just mentioned—being again exposed to the day. The crown of the arch, in fact, had been denuded off, while its buttresses were left in the lower ground on either side of the old anticlinal axis. The core of the anticlinal consists of rocks that, on the whole, withstood denudation much better than the less durable rocks in which that core had at one time been enveloped. Under the action of denudation the lowering proceeded, therefore, at a differential rate; the more durable rocks remaining in higher relief as the Pentland Hills, while the less durable Carboniferous strata give rise to the plains on their flanks.

PENTLAND SILURIAN ROCKS—FOSSILS.

As it is with the rocks composing the old core that we are now especially concerned, their history may be noticed in somewhat greater detail. The rocks composing the floor upon which the Carboniferous strata were deposited consist partly of Silurian rocks, partly of others belonging to the Old Red Sandstone Series. The Pentland Silurian Rocks are of Wenlock-Ludlow age, and may be described as a series of shales or argillites with subordinate beds of flagstone, sandstone, and even conglomerate, the whole being much plicated, deeply denuded, and unconformably overlain by different members of the Old Red Sandstone Series. These rocks have yielded a considerable number of Eurypterids, as well as other invertebrata chiefly of a Ludlow facies. A good collection of them is exhibited in the Geological Survey Collection placed in the Royal Scottish Museum at Edinburgh. Another collection of fossils from the same beds also exists in the Natural History Section of the same Museum. Amongst the numerous private collections from the Pentland Silurian rocks may be especially mentioned that belonging to the late Dr David Hardie of Bavelaw Castle, now in the Edinburgh Museum. Most of the Silurian rocks of this area are of unequivocally marine origin ; but the occurrence here and there amongst them of flagstones showing desiccation cracks would appear to indicate that lagoon conditions had occasionally begun to alternate with those of the more open sea towards the close of the Ludlow period. It is not surprising, therefore, that in places these Ludlow rocks should be found to graduate upwards into strata which in lithological character, relative position, and included fossils, correspond to the Downtonian series of Lanarkshire. Only a few small and detached remnants of these rocks occur in the Pentland area, chiefly around the headwaters of the rivers Lyne and Esk.

Considerable disturbance followed the close of the period under notice. The Silurian strata were compressed into a very close series of N.N.E. and S.S.W. folds, whose flanks are inclined at very high angles, and often inverted. At a later period denudation effected the removal of many thousands of feet of strata, so as elsewhere to expose the underlying rocks down to those of Arenig age, or even to others more ancient still.

CONGLOMERATES AND SANDSTONES.

In the area specially under notice, a thick series of conglomerates and sandstones was afterwards laid down upon the denuded surface thus formed. These form the local base of the Lower division of the Old Red Sandstone series. Concurrently with the deposition of these rocks of aqueous origin, some volcanic cones came into existence within what is now the Pentland area. These were doubtless of small size at the outset, but were destined ultimately to assume much more imposing proportions. Volcanic products arising from these cones were mingled in variable proportions with the other constituents of the conglomerates, which contain rolled fragments of lavas derived from these sources, and are locally interstratified with beds of tuff. The bulk of the conglomerate, however, consists of well-rounded fragments of the Highland Metamorphic Rocks, of Arenig Radiolarian Cherts, of the Haggis Rock, of various greywackes, quartzites, and argillites of later date, and, lastly, of some remarkable masses of fossiliferous limestone. The age of the greater part of the materials composing the conglomerate hardly admits of question ; but that of the limestone blocks has long been a matter of controversy. The late Dr Davidson thought that some of the Brachiopoda they contain were not unlike those of the Devonian rocks ; while the abundance of *Favosites* and other corals prevalent in rocks of Devonian age gives to polished specimens of these derived blocks of limestone a facies which at once recalls that of the well-known limestones of Torquay. But the balance of evidence is considered by many to be in favour of the view that the limestone came direct from some of the rocks composing the platform upon which the conglomerates unconformably lie. A good series of fossils obtained from the limestones in question is exhibited in the Geological Survey Collection.

In Monk's Burn (Route 6), these Pentland conglomerates are apparently nearly 2000 feet in thickness, and they are clearly seen to graduate upward through ashy sandstones into a series of tuffs and lavas.

VOLCANIC ROCKS.

The ashy bands occurring on different platforms in this conglomerate, mark some of the more violent eruptions of the volcanoes already mentioned as having previously come into existence near. The exact site of the vents cannot be determined with accuracy ; but the succession of the volcanic rocks that emanated from them has been made out clearly. These may be denoted by numerals as follows : (1) The lowest lavas of Warklaw Hill which are of a basaltic and andesitic type. (2) An acid series.

(3) A second basaltic and andesitic series, which forms the lowest bed exposed on the south-east side of a large fault at Loganlee. (4) A series of tuffs, followed by felsites, trachytes, and acid andesites, some showing beautiful perlitic structure, and others well-marked rhyolitic banding. These rocks will be seen between the summit of Carnethy and that of Scald Law. (5) A third series of basalts, andesites, and tuffs. Amongst these occur the beautiful "porphyrite" of Carnethy, well known to collectors of volcanic rocks. This can be examined on the south-east flanks of the Pentlands, at no great distance from the great boundary fault which limits the Carboniferous rocks of the Dalkeith Coalfield. The aggregate thickness of the Pentland Volcanic rocks exceeds, rather than falls short of, 6000 feet. A good series of specimens of all the chief varieties is exhibited in the Survey Collections already mentioned.

At a late period in the development of the volcanic rocks, one of the columns of molten felsite rose within its cone to such a height that the pressure exerted upon its supporting walls was much greater than they could bear. As a consequence, some intrusions of molten rock took place far beneath the surface. At one point a thick sheet of molten rock of acid composition ate its way between the Silurian strata and the Lower Old Red Conglomerates overlying them. This "laccolite" now forms the Black Hill. As the intrusion proceeded, the invaded conglomerates underwent a considerable amount of induration.

VOLCANIC NECKS.

Three small volcanic necks are found piercing the basic lavas of group 3, a little to the west of Swanston. These are partly filled in with acid agglomerate and rhyolitic felsite, and probably supplied material to the platform of acid lavas and tuffs of group 4, out of which is carved the chain of hills, of which Caerketton, Castlelaw, and Scald Law are some of the most prominent tops. The occurrence of these necks supports the suggestion of Maclaren and Sir Archibald Geikie, that the great focus of distribution of the Pentland volcanic rocks lay to the north of the range, now buried under newer strata. These rocks may represent the conduits of small parasitic cones.

UPPER OLD RED SANDSTONE.

The close of the volcanic episode was followed by a period of disturbance, of which one of the results was that the newly formed volcanic rocks were tilted towards the east and the south-east; and it is possible that some of the faults now traversing these rocks may have also come into existence at the same time. Afterwards came a prolonged period of denudation, which swept off from some parts of the Pentlands, especially on their western side, the whole of the volcanic rocks of the middle division of the Old Red Sandstone series, as well as a considerable thickness of the older rocks.

At the base of the Carboniferous System lies the Upper Old Red Sandstone. This is violently unconformable to the Old Red Sandstone rocks of the Pentland area; while these are in turn unconformable to a greater extent upon the rocks which were formerly regarded as the Lower Old Red Sandstone—that is to say, the grits which here and in Lanarkshire and Ayrshire conformably overlie the Upper Ludlow rock, but which from their contained fish fauna have been proved by the Geological Survey to be of Downtonian age. There are thus two extensive unconformities in the strata once classed as Old Red Sandstone; and it is chiefly within the Pentland area where the relationship of each of these to the others can be clearly made out.

CARBONIFEROUS STRATA.

The Upper Old Red Sandstone passes up conformably into the Lower Carboniferous Strata which in places overlap on to the still older rocks on which they in consequence lie unconformably.

GEOLOGICAL FEATURES SEEN ON BALERNO RAILWAY.

The foregoing outline of the history of the rocks may now be followed by a sketch of the chief features observable along the routes of journeys from Edinburgh outward.

The railway from Edinburgh to Balerno traverses the north-west flank of the Pentlands nearly along the local strike of the Carboniferous rocks, which here belong to various horizons lower than the Oil Shales. Near Edinburgh the railway follows the outcrop of strata a few hundred feet above the horizon of the volcanic rocks of Arthur's Seat, while near Balerno the strata are well below that horizon. The rising-ground between Balerno Station and the foot of the Pentland Hills consists of Lower Carboniferous strata, which dip from the hills at a higher angle than the slope of the ground. Successively, lower rocks therefore tend to rise to the surface as we approach the higher ground. At Bavelaw Castle the base of the Upper Old Red Sandstone rises to the surface, and Silurian rocks appear beyond ; all the strata of age intermediate between these two having been swept away in pre-carboniferous times.

SILURIAN ROCKS AT BAVELAW.

Just outside Bavelaw Castle there are two small quarries in the Silurian rocks. Some small sub-basic dykes occur here. The absence of cleavage, the high inclination of the strata, and their comparatively soft nature are the chief points to be noted. The green mudstones of these quarries have yielded a suite of fossils of Wenlock facies.

Following the path eastward, several exposures of the same rocks will be observed. One of these Silurian outcrops on the left will be seen directly capped by a small outlier of volcanic rock belonging to the Pentland Series ; while on the right other exposures of these highly contorted Silurian strata will be seen to be surmounted by the gently inclined rocks of Upper Old Red Sandstone which form Hare Hill.

After a traverse of a few hundred yards, we reach the outcrop of a great intrusive mass of felsite or micro-granite which has been already referred to as having eaten its way between the Silurian strata and the Old Red Conglomerates that underlie the volcanic rocks. Near the waterfall at Logan Burn the induration produced by the felsite at its junction with the conglomerates may be observed; while nearer Loganlee the evidence of the intrusive contact of the same rock with the Silurian strata can easily be seen.

ON CARNETHY.

At Loganlee there is a choice of routes : one over the volcanic rocks of Carnethy to Penicuik; the other, up Logan Burn, past the conical hills of lava known as the Kips, down Monk's Burn, to Nine-Mile-Burn and Blackhill.

The journey by way of Carnethy is at first across a powerful fault, which brings down the lavas of No. 3 platform against the Silurian strata of Loganlee. These lavas are chiefly basic and sub-acid in composition, and can be examined in several quarries and natural exposures on the way up the hillside. Just beyond the hill-top we come upon a zone of tuffs, which we find to be, as we travel eastward, succeeded by a fine group of lavas of more acid composition than those below; these acid and subacid lavas comprising some good examples of perlitic, and, locally, of rhyolitic structure. These are well seen between Carnethy and Scald Law. The light-coloured tuff beds are here in places filled in with small spheres (once hollow), evidently produced by rain drops upon the newly fallen ashes similar to those at present found after showers upon the ashes of Vesuvius.

On the eastern slopes of Carnethy there are abundant opportunities for collecting good specimens of the Carnethy Porphyrite (of group 5) exhibiting a considerable variety of structures. Beyond the quarries where this rock occurs the low ground consists of rock of Carboniferous age, here let down by the great boundary fault which flanks that side of the Pentland Hills, from Carlops nearly to Portobello.

BY THE KIPS TO NINE-MILE-BURN.

The Conglomerates belonging to the Lower Division of the Old Red Sandstone may be observed in Logan Burn, their varied constituents noted, and their excessive induration near the junction with the felsite. Good specimens of the Arenig Radiolarian

Cherts occur, as do large masses of jasper, etc. The Upper Old Red Conglomerates and Sandstones may also be seen, largely made up of resorted materials derived from the strata below, and reposing unconformably upon the Lower Division. Then the large fault seen at Loganlee can again be crossed ; and we find ourselves on the andesitic lava forming the Kips. Here and there the lavas are parted by thin bands of tuff or of conglomerate. Crossing now to the head of Monk's Burn, we have on our right smooth, rounded grassy hills composed of Silurian strata ; while on our left is a repetition of the older conglomerate group whose lower members are seen at Logan Burn. As we follow the burn downward, we may examine good sections of the Silurian strata, afterwards followed by the conglomerates and ashy sandstones which here form the basement member of the Pentland Old Red rocks, as these latter are carried down by their high south-easterly dip. Near the top of the series the percentage of ashy matter mixed with the conglomerate and sandstone shows a gradual increase, until these rocks pass upwards into veritable tuffs, which in their turn are succeeded by the lava-flows of the Kips. Near Nine-Mile-Burn the great boundary fault crosses, and the low ground before us consists of Carboniferous rocks including the Dalkeith Coalfield, which was mapped more than forty years ago by Mr Howell.

CHAPTER XV.

The Balm Well—Burdiehouse Limestone—Pentland Shale—Glaciation—Reindeer Cave—Development of the Pentlands—Formation of the Pentland Passes—Loganlee and Glencorse Valley—Influence of the Ice Sheet—Period of Maximum Glaciation—Retreat of the Ice Sheet—Pentland Passes—Pass between Pentlands and Braids—Retreat of Southern Upland Ice—Post-Glacial Denudation.

THE first part of the way skirts the north-eastern slopes of the Braid Hills and the Pentland ridge, and crosses a patch of the red sandstones and conglomerates that form the Upper Old Red Sandstone of the region, and rest in violent unconformability on the Lower Old Red Sandstone volcanic series, of which the greater part of the Pentland range is composed. Passing Liberton and Alnwickhill, the site of the Edinburgh Corporation Waterworks, a halt may be called at St Katherine's or the Balm Well, a spring which rises on the line of the great Pentland fault, about three-quarters of a mile south of Liberton. The water in this well is covered with a film of petroleum, derived no doubt from the bituminous matter in the upper or Oil Shale group of the Calciferous Sandstone series that forms the low ground on the east or downthrow side of the fault. The Balm Well was held in great veneration in pre-Reformation days as a healing spring for various diseases. The tradition is that the well sprang from some of the oil brought by St Catherine from Mount Sinai to St Margaret having been spilt on the spot. Cromwell's soldiers in 1650 closed the well; it was afterwards re-opened.

Immediately south of St Catherine's the road passes the hamlet of Kaimes, where may be seen one of the long gravel ridges known over Scotland as a Kaim—a designation now generally adopted, not in Scotland alone, but by glacialists in other countries, for such relics of the Great Ice Age. The next place of interest that is passed is Burdiehouse, a corruption of Bordeaux House, one of the numerous place-names of French origin that are found scattered through the Lothians.

BURDIEHOUSE LIMESTONE—PENTLAND SHALE.

The Burdiehouse Limestone, which has been worked here for many years, is celebrated for its rich array of estuarine shells, fish and plant remains, and may be examined in the line of old quarries along its outcrop near the road. At Straiton, a short distance further on, the Pentland Oil Works are to be seen. The petroleum which is produced here is obtained by distillation from the Pentland Shale, a seam of oil shale that occurs about 150 feet above the Burdiehouse Limestone in the Oil Shale series. The strata here are steeply inclined to the E.S.E., and in part of the shale workings the seam was found to have been thrown completely on end, and even slightly inverted by the lateral pressure accompanying the upheaval of the Pentland ridge. Good sections of the steep strata associated with the Oil Shales are to be seen in the Bilston Burn, as well as the whole Carboniferous Limestone series, with the Edge Coals right up to the Roslyn Sandstone. At Glencorse, the farm road to Castlelaw may be followed. Immediately above Castlelaw farm, a halt may be called at the ancient fort, the lines of which are still discernible. At this point the rocks are dark slaggy andesites dipping to the south-east, which become gradually more acid as we cross the strike and move northwards. At the top of Castlelaw, a hill 1595 feet in height, fine examples may be seen of brecciated acid lavas. The acid beds are generally heath-covered, and coincide with the hollows or coombs, a small example of which occurs on the west side of the summit of Castlelaw Hill. The view from the more prominent heathy ridges is very fine, embracing as it does a varied undulating expanse of rich farmland, wood, and hill, with towns and villages and the glistening waters of the Firth of Forth in the far distance. Immediately in front, on the opposite slope of the hills beyond Glencorse Burn, is to be seen the site of the Battle of Rullion Green (see Route 1). The path traverses the hillside overlooking the romantic old mansion-house of Woodhouselee, the residence of the distinguished Tytler family. On the west, in the bottom of the glen, the picturesque reservoir of Glencorse winds round the bases of the hills.

GLACIATION.

The whole of the Pentland range bears traces of intense glaciation; and ice marks have been found on the top of Allermuir Hill, over 1500 feet above sea level, showing that at one period the great ice sheet was so thick as to completely override the range. By examining the boulder clay on the slopes and in the valleys, it will be found that in addition to stones of local origin, there are also Highland schists and other rocks, all of which have travelled eastwards along the direction pointed out by the ice scratches on the solid rock below. As Allermuir summit is not far from the path, it may be climbed by any one who wishes to see the view; but equally good views may be obtained from the path all the way down to Dreghorn. On crossing the flat top of the range, a grand panorama of the Lothians, Fife, and the upper part of the Firth of Forth, with the blue Highland hills in the distance, opens out before the spectator.

REINDEER CAVE.

After looking into the deep cleft of Howden Glen, on the other side may be seen the Hundred Steps formed by the late R. A. Macfie, of Dreghorn, down the steep hillside. At the foot of the steps, on passing round the foot of Greencraig on the right, the interesting Reindeer Cleft can be examined (see Route 2). This is a fissure about two feet broad in the red porphyrite cliffs, in which Mr Macfie discovered in 1886 a quantity of bones of the reindeer, horse, wolf, fox, and other animals, covered by rock debris, and partly cemented together by a calcareous deposit. Some of the bones showed signs of having been gnawed by some animal, probably a hyæna, which may have had its den here in early post-glacial times.

DEVELOPMENT OF THE PENTLANDS.

The platform of Silurian and Lower Old Red Sandstone rocks, upon which the Upper Old Red Sandstone and the Carboniferous strata were laid down, in the area now under consideration, was an uneven one, and was already, in Pre-Carboniferous times, a rising ground, as proved by the outliers of Lower Carboniferous strata resting directly upon the older rocks at Bonaly reservoir to the north, and near West Linton to the south. A further consideration of the relations of the Carboniferous rocks to those of Lower Old Red Sandstone ages also points to the prevalent south-easterly dip of the latter rocks having been in great part established before the former were laid down on their denuded edges. But, from what has been already stated, it follows that the present Pentlands owe their existence to the Post-Carboniferous folding and faulting, and more especially to the superior resisting power of the core of older rocks, to those of their enveloping Carboniferous strata in the subsequent prodigiously long period or periods during which they have been subjected to subaerial denudation. A study of the streams which traverse these hills reveals some of the stages in this process. Most of these streams take their rise near the north-west edge of the range, and flow southwards or eastwards; some even rising on the comparatively low ground to the north-west of the hills, and flowing right back eastwards into the hills in comparatively matured valleys across the axis of the range. Only a few flow to northwards and westwards, and have a short and steep descent into streams that have a much less distance to traverse to reach the sea than those that drain southwards and eastwards.

FORMATION OF THE PENTLAND PASSES.

This distribution at once shows that the main streams which flow eastward had their rise in the area now representing the plain to the north and west of the range occupied by Carboniferous or perhaps younger rocks; or even still further to the north, the strata having been entirely removed by denudation to produce the existing plain. The transverse passes which form so conspicuous a feature of the Pentlands are thus to be accounted for as having been sunk in the hills by streams of much greater volume than those at present draining them, and which have been beheaded by the production of the northern plain. The Ochils and the Campsie Fells are also volcanic platforms, surrounded by softer sedimentary strata and isolated by denudation. They are also traversed by a similar series of transverse passes produced by rivers that have been beheaded towards the north, and truncated to the south by streams working along the strike in softer strata. In the case of the Pentlands the beheadal of the streams on the north and west is complete, but on the south and east only the Esk, towards the north end of the area, and the Medwyn-Clyde at the south end, have affected the stealing away of the streams ; while the Lyne is the only stream which has been enabled to continue its south-east course across the intervening hollow, filled with softer strata, between the Pentlands and the Southern Uplands, to join the Tweed, and reach the sea after a very long course. The same story of capture and beheadal of streams along the margin of the Southern Uplands is everywhere patent, the Nith and Lyne-Tweed being the only two streams which pass from the northern plain and cross the Southern Upland Hills.

FORMATION OF LOGANLEE AND GLENCORSE VALLEY —INFLUENCE OF THE ICE SHEET.

These passes, due to streams deriving their volume from a much larger catchment basin than that of the present Pentlands, are mainly across the strike of the rocks or the "grain of the country." Their primary tributaries necessarily run along the strike of the weaker strata or along "shatter belts" caused by the faults. The valley in which the upper part of the Glencorse Reservoir and the Loganlee Reservoir lie is of this nature, and partly coincides with the outcrop of basic lavas of group 3 and some associated sedimentary strata, flanked on each side by outcrops of more resisting acid lavas and ashes and intrusive rocks. The cutting of the upper end of the valley has been assisted by the shattering of the rocks that accompanied the great longitudinal fault which is already referred to as occurring there.

To the action of the smaller secondary tributaries which necessarily cut the "grain of the country" is to be attributed the isolation of the tops along the more resisting acid volcanic platforms.

As will be seen in the sequel, the Pentlands show evidence of having been powerfully affected in Post-Tertiary time by the passage of the ice sheet during the maximum glaciation, and of the "melt-waters" from the ice during the stages of its disappearance. The action of the streams in Post-Glacial time is shown, by the cuttings in the boulder clay which chokes such valleys as those entering from the north into Glencorse Reservoir, to be trifling indeed compared to that already accomplished in Pre-Glacial time.

PERIOD OF MAXIMUM GLACIATION.

The direction of the striæ found on the summit of Allermuir, the plentiful occurrence of Highland and other boulders, within the Pentland Hills, derived from sources outside the area, and also the distribution of the boulder clay, all point to these hills having been completely overridden by an ice sheet having its origin within the West Highlands. After crossing to the east side of the hills the ice then coalesced with another ice stream emanating from the Southern Uplands and continued to flow onward in a south easterly direction, crossing the Lammermoors on its way to the east of England, and leaving a train of boulders of Highland schists and rocks derived from the central valley of Scotland, to mark its course. It was during this phase of the Glaciation that all pre-existing talus and other superficial deposits were removed from the area and swept forward by the ice, and used by it as the graving and polishing tools that gave the characteristic rounded flowing outline to these hills, over-steepened their opposing faces, accentuated the outcrops of lava flows, and fluted crests and ridges in the direction of this ice movement, the boulder clay or moraine profonde of this ice sheet now flooring the sheltered hollows, especially the valleys, with a southern aspect, being almost wholly made up of such tools, worn and blunted, and scored and polished, set in a matrix of rock-filings or rockflour.

RETREAT OF THE ICE-SHEET.

Towards the close of the period, however, there came a time when the northern ice had so far dwindled that it could no longer overtop the Pentland Hills, but could still abut against their north-western flanks. At the same time, the less powerful ice-sheet from the Southern Uplands, though also much dwindled, being no longer opposed by the northern stream, was able to reach their south-eastern flanks. The greater part of the Pentlands, and a considerable area of the lower ground to the north-east, was therefore free from ice. At first the ice from the northern stream pushed its lobes through the passes into the Pentland valleys, thus helping to abrade and lower their beds, but on a further decrease the surface of the ice-sheet was only able to reach the level of the watersheds at the head of the passes, and large volumes of water, liberated from the melting ice, escaped across the cols and passes, and flowed through the Pentland valleys on to the open ground to the north-east, where it was in part pounded back by the continuation eastwards of the northern ice, preventing its escape into what is now the Firth of Forth. The great floods thus let loose formed streams, the course of which was determined by the margin of the ice, for owing to radiation of heat from the bare ground, and also to the fact that the marginal ice is usually more soil-laden than that of the body of the glacier, it absorbs the sun's heat more readily and disappears faster than the purer ice. Running therefore nearly parallel with the contour lines of the hills, and being abundantly supplied with moramic materials, the streams soon incised their beds in the projecting rocky spurs of the hills that obstructed their course, graded up with sand and gravel their less steep reaches, and expanded into temporary lakes in hollows, which they wholly or partially silted up, and eventually escaped through the first pass encountered along their course. To the first cause are to be attributed the sharp, steep-pointed rocky cuts so often found crossing the crests of projecting spurs of the hills, and the origin of which was for long considered to be inexplicable. To the other causes are to be relegated the origin of the large spreads of gravels, sands, and silts that are found on the northern flanks of the Pentland and Braid Hills, as in the hollow west of Bavelaw Castle, and at Comiston near Edinburgh. Marking three successive stages in the decrease of the ice are to be found concentric ridges of gravelly material in the hollows south-west of Bavelaw Castle, each corresponding with a rock notch in the spur of the hill which bounds the pass leading over to the Loganlee reservoir. The passage of this great volume of debris-laden water across the col no doubt helped still further to lower the sill of the pass and to "overdeepen" the main valley, which is steep-sided and out of harmony with the side streams, so that they all flow steeply down into it, and one, the Logan Burn, now carrying a much greater volume of water than the main stream, leaps down into the main valley over a series of waterfalls at the foot of a deep cañon, above which the valley bottom is of very gentle gradient for a long way back. That an agent no longer at work has been concerned in cutting the pass higher up is abundantly proved by the cones of debris brought down by the side streams being greater than the streams in the pass valley is able to distribute, and the actual watershed between the streams flowing north to the Bavelaw reservoir, and south to that of Loganlee, is formed by such a cone, which thus constitutes a corrom,* and shows that the side stream has at different times flowed either way.

PENTLAND PASSES.

To the east of Bavelaw a second or lower pass between the Black Hill and Bell's Hill on which rise streams flowing respectively north-west into Thriepmuir, and south-east into Glencorse reservoirs. Both streams rise in a peat moss or alluvial flat on the bottom of the pass which constitutes the present watershed,

---

* From a Gaelic word Cothrom (pronounced Corrom), meaning a chance or balance, and in use in Argyleshire for alluvial cones similarly situated. The word phonetically spelled is adopted by Messrs P. F. Kendall and E. B. Bailey in their paper on the Giaciation of East Lothian. Trans. Roy. Soc. Edin. 1908, Vol. xlvi., Pt. 1 (separate part).

thus showing that they had no action in the production of the pass, which doubtless had a similar origin to that of Bavelaw, and was probably the main trunk of the beheaded river.

This pass seems to have served, after the disuse of the Bavelaw pass through shrinkage of the ice, for a long period for the escape of the marginal water of the Northern Glacier. As a consequence of this drainage, and as also that of the higher pass, the central valley of this part of the Pentlands appears to have been greatly denuded of boulder clay, and a considerable flood-plain of gravel laid down. On the south side of the Pentlands, below the opening of the Glencorse valley, there are abundant gravels and sands which are probably due to the arresting of the glacial streams emanating from the hills and flowing over a much less steep gradient.

PASS BETWEEN PENTLANDS AND BRAIDS.

The passes to the east of that just mentioned are much higher, and, if they ever were used for the escape of marginal water, could only have been for a very short period, and were soon relieved by the last mentioned one, and of the wide pass between the Pentlands and the Braid Hills to the east. These valleys, into which they lead, are therefore still much encumbered with boulder clay, the amount of which has been cut away being no more than can be accounted for by the streams which at present occupy them. Such, however, appears not to have been the case with the wide col between the Pentlands and the Braids. Large volumes of the melt water seems to have flowed over it, and to have given rise to the vast spreads of sands and gravels now found on the east of it.

RETREAT OF SOUTHERN UPLAND ICE.

The ice of the Southern Uplands has left similar evidence of its retreat from the south-east flanks of the Pentlands, but in this case the phenomena are marginal. These are well displayed in the area between West Linton and Glencorse. Many of the streams on emerging from the hills, instead of following the natural slope of the land, follow more or less the contour lines, and form gorges, one of the best examples being the North Esk and its tributaries on both sides of Carlops, of which the well-known Habbie's How is part. A little further to the east is the burn which passes Walton, which, for a good distance, runs parallel with a long ridge or "Kaim" of glacial gravel evidently laid down in a marginal channel of which ice formed one side, that, on melting, has caused the glacial deposits which choked the channel to assume the form of a chain of mounds.

The outlying spur on the Pentlands, which juts out near Rullion Green, is traversed by dry rock-notches making overflow channels of the marginal waters obstructed by the spur, and from these notches ridges of sand and gravel are found passing down to meet the gravels emanating from the Glencorse valley, and to join with the wide spread of similar detrital matter spread over the greater part of the area to the south and east left by the retreating Southern Upland ice, whose waters were obstructed from flowing northwards by the Forth Glacier, and which were obliged to overflow in places into the Tyne valley. The difference between the gravel on this side of the hills and that on the north is the great preponderance of stones, the original source of which is to be found within the Southern Uplands, while these are absent from the gravels on the north side.

POST-GLACIAL DENUDATION.

As already stated, the action of the streams in the Pentland area since glacial times has been comparatively slight. In such cases as those where the valleys had been floored with a coating of boulder clay or glacial gravel, only a small proportion of these comparatively loosely compacted superficial deposits has been removed, and in a few instances only has the old rocky floor of the valleys been reached by the streams.

The notches cut in the rocks by the side streams and hills are only faintly incised, and the "cones of dejection" of debris, left at their junction with the main streams, owing to the sudden loss of gradient, are small. The alluvial flats bordering the main water-courses show the inability of these streams to do more than distribute the debris brought down into them by the side streams. For the same reason they are all made to meander, and thus occasionally to reach their side bluffs and saw into and remove the glacial deposits, the talus, or even the shattered rocks, of which they may consist, and to produce crescent-shaped steep-sided cuts, raw and bare while the stream remains at their base, but soon grassed over as the bed of the stream moves onwards.

The effects of frost are best shown on the rock faces of the hills oversteepened by ice in the way some of the escarpments are draped or petticoated with screes of talus, which assuming the angles of rest of debris help to renew the graceful and pleasing concave curves to the hill slopes, the whole tendency of prolonged glaciation having been to produce the opposite type of curve.

The Pentlands, consisting for the most part of a pile of volcanic rocks, which are much jointed and porous, absorb a considerable proportion of the rainfall. The chemical constitution of these rocks imparts to the water during its underground course such ingredients as to make it a most desirable drinking water. Most of this water reappears as springs along the sides and bottoms of the valleys, and its good qualities having been long known, have caused it to be impounded in numerous reservoirs and distributed to Edinburgh and the surrounding towns and villages. For this reason the whole drainage of this part of the area is strictly regulated.

The water from a great part of the remaining Pentland areas, where the rocks are chiefly of sedimentary origin, is of inferior quality, but is also impounded to afford compensation to the streams depleted for drinking purposes. But it is with the reservoirs, as affording the means of estimating the rate of denudation effected by the " degrading " agencies at work in their respective catchment basins, that we are chiefly concerned. In dry seasons, when the water is low, the amount of silting up of these basins is seen to be considerable, and is especially evident towards the head of the Glencorse reservoir.

And the effect of this impounding of the water is to show how comparatively rapid is the action of even the puny waves, raised in these narrow and confined ponds, in assorting the screes of loose debris, accumulated on what was formerly hillside, and even in cutting into live rock, as evidenced by the raw scars which fringe the steeper margins of the dams where not artificially protected. The water engineers could readily calculate the decreasing capacity of the reservoirs, and thus afford an estimate of their yearly silting up, which would form an index of the amount abstracted in the solid form from off the general surface of the catchment basin. They could likewise easily calculate the amount carried off in solution.

CHAPTER XVI.

ORNITHOLOGY OF THE PENTLANDS.

THE Pentlands do not show any remarkable features of bird life which would attract naturalists from afar to visit them. Like other Scottish ranges they have lost and found in bird life—the gamekeeper has decimated destructive species and birds of prey, and given an artificial protection to game birds, ducks, and other smaller kinds which fall into the larger class of the pursued.

The Pentlands have been visited from time to time by rare species, which have halted there on migration. Such were the troupe of rough-legged buzzards which visited the head of Logan-lee some years ago. Such are occasional visitors like the ruff, immature of course, one of which fell to the gun of a sportsman. In the following list of birds, only those are given which remain on the hill to breed, or are such frequent and steady visitors as to come under the notice of the occasional pedestrian. All in the list are breeding species, except those marked thus *, which are winter visitors, and those thus †, regular visitors, which do not breed.

Missel Thrush.	Jackdaw.
Song Thrush.	Magpie.
Blackbird.	
*Fieldfare.	Skylark.
*Redwing.	
Ring Ousel.	Swift.
Wheatear.	
Redstart.	Cuckoo.
Redbreast.	
Stonechat.	Tawny Owl.

Whinchat.

Sedge Warbler.
Wood Warbler
Willow Warbler.
Whitethroat.
Garden Warbler.
Gold Crest.

Hedge Accentor.

Water Ousel or Dipper.

Cole Tit.
Great Tit.
Blue Tit.
Marsh Tit.

Wren.

Treecreeper.

Pied Wagtail.
Grey Wagtail.
Meadow Pipit.
Tree Pipit.

Spotted Flycatcher.

Martin.
Swallow.
Sand Martin.

Sparrow.
Chaffinch.
Greenfinch.
Bullfinch.

Barn Owl.
Long Eared Owl.
*Short Eared Owl.

Kestrel.
Merlin.
Sparrow Hawk.
*Peregrine Falcon.

†Heron.
*Cormorant.

Mallard : Wild Duck.
*Goldeneye.
Teal Duck.
Tufted Duck.
*Pochard.
*Widgeon.

Ring Dove.
Stock Dove.

Coot.
Water Hen.
Corncrake.
*Water Rail.

Black Grouse.
Grouse.
Pheasant.
Partridge.

Golden Plover.
Green Plover or Lapwing.
Woodcock.
Common Snipe.
Redshank.

Linnet.
*Brambling.

Reed Bunting.
Yellow Hammer.
Common Bunting.
*Snow Bunting.

Starling.

Rook.
Carrion Crow.

Common Sandpiper.
Dunlin.
Curlew.
*Jack Snipe.

Black Headed Gull.
†Herring Gull.
†Common Gull.
†Lesser Black Backed Gull.

Little Grebe.

BIBLIOGRAPHY.

[All the after-noted works have something either in biography, history, fiction, or topography which connects them with our subject.]

Pocket Flora of Edinburgh and District. By C. O. Sonntag. (For Botany.)

Annals of Penicuik. By J. W. Wilson.

The Water of Leith from Source to Sea. By John Geddie.

Reminiscences. By Charles Cowan (privately printed).

Memoirs of the Life of Sir John Clerk of Penicuik. (Scottish History Society.)

Liberton in Ancient and Modern Times. By George Good.

Castellated and Domestic Architecture of Scotland. By M'Gibbon and Ross.

Life and Letters of W. B. Hodgson. Edited by J. M. D. Meiklejohn.

Memoir of George Meikle Kemp. By T. Bonnar.

Memoir of Patrick Fraser Tytler. By J. W. Burgon.

The Woodhouselee MS. Edited by C. E. S. Chambers.

Edinburgh and its Neighbourhood. By Hugh Miller.

Walks near Edinburgh. By Margaret Warrender.

Edinburgh and District Water Supply. By James Colston.

Scottish Rivers. By Sir T. Dick Lauder.

Biggar and the House of Fleming. By William Hunter.

Horæ Subsecivæ, 1st Series. By John Brown, M.D.

Castles and Mansions of the Lothians. By John Small, LL.D.

Thirteen Engravings of Scenery of Gentle Shepherd around Carlops, and with portrait of Allan Ramsay. (No title or publisher's name).

The Pentland Hills, their Paths and Passes. By W. A. S.

The Pentland Rising and Rullion Green. By Charles Sanford Terry.

The Pentland Rising. By R. L. Stevenson.

Memories and Portraits. By R. L. Stevenson.

Edinburgh—Picturesque Notes. By R. L. Stevenson.

Memorials. By Henry Cockburn.

Journal. By Henry Cockburn.

Biographical Annals of the Parish of Colinton. By Thomas Murray.

The Parish of Colinton. By David Shankie.

Transactions of the Edinburgh Architectural Association. Vol. 3 (for Bavelaw and St Katherine's).

Johnston of Warriston. By William Morrison. (Famous Scots Series.)

Cromwell's Scotch Campaigns, 1650-51. By W. S. Douglas.

Also articles in *Chambers's Journal* on "The Skirts of the Pentlands" (1903); "Haunted Woodhouselee" (1905); and "Popularity of Robert Louis Stevenson" (1905); "Cromwell before Edinburgh, 1650" (*Scottish Review*, October 1905); "Some Pentland Memories" (*Scotsman*, July 6, 1907); "Memories of Old Morningside" (*Scotsman*, October 12, 1907): "The Padre in Scotland," in *Singapore Free Press* (1904-6), by Rev. George M. Reith.

POETRY AND FICTION.

The Gentle Shepherd. By Allan Ramsay.

Ballads and Songs by David Mallet. Edited by F. Dinsdale.

Poems in the Scottish Dialect. By James Thomson, Weaver in Kenleith (1801).

Poems. By James Ballantine.

The Miller of Deanhaugh. By James Ballantine.

Harry Ogilvie. By James Grant.

Weir of Hermiston. By R. L. Stevenson.

St Ives. By R. L. Stevenson.

John Burnet of Barns. By John Buchan.

The Martyr Shepherd. By R. H. Moncrieff.

13/2

EDINBURGH :
PRINTED BY DAVID MACDONALD, 74 HANOVER STREET.